LIVING QUESTIONS TO DEAD GODS

LIVING QUESTIONS TO DEAD GODS

JACQUES DURANDEAUX

TRANSLATED BY WILLIAM WHITMAN

with an Introduction by
GABRIEL VAHANIAN

SHEED AND WARD: NEW YORK

CONTENTS

CONTENTS

Introduction

NO GOD is worshipped who does not die. The God by whom all things are explained is in turn explained by them. And if no speech is possible without God, nothing is said, however, unless God is a euphemism for silence. On the one hand, there is thus no God but the one who is the product of our imagination. On the other hand, there is no God that cannot be imagined, or else God could not truly be *nothing but* the product of our imagination: he could not be the truth of our imagination.

The dilemma which confronts us today was concretely faced by Dostoyevsky. In *The Brothers Karamazov* he wrote: "There would have been no civilization if they had not invented God." But in the notebooks to *The Possessed* he admits that there is no question other than the question whether it is possible for civilized man to believe. What else can man do but return the compliment to the God who created him? What can he do but kill him? Reduced to our images of him, and these images being no longer serviceable, God must die. But when God is dead, and an entire civilization collapses at the same time, as Jacques Durandeaux points out, what nevertheless remains is the problem of God.

Rather than removing the problem, the contention that God is merely a cultural phenomenon makes it inescapable. True enough, it may be that instead of being a mystery, as in the Christian epoch of Western civilization, the reality of God now merely becomes a problem—at best. And it is equally true, as Marx and Freud have shown, that our traditional arsenal of religious attitudes actually consisted of attitudes that were not religious only. They were the laudable yet pitiful attempt to mask man's alienation, his obsessions, or his illusions. Indeed, nothing less than the death of God could begin to redeem man from them. "The criticisms of Marx and Freud are sound," writes Durandeaux, without any kind of afterthought as is usually the case with religious thinkers who even sympathetically grapple with this aspect of the question; and he adds without fear of denuding his own argument to the point of perhaps invalidating it *a priori,* "A certain debunking of religious practices has succeeded. A good number of ostensibly 'religious' responses have been shown to be other than they were thought to be. The religious realities to which they were supposed to correspond turned out to be not specifically religious."

What this means, however, should not be lost from our sight merely for the sake of one kind of new positivism or another. That in the past Christians generally acquiesced all too easily in some sort of positivism or revelation, as Bonhoeffer would say, is today no excuse for eluding the problem which lay at its roots. For, as Marx himself admits, the transference of which religion is the soothing expression is really rooted in what actually alienates man: it does not and cannot obliterate this alienation. It can only transfer it. But, Durandeaux writes,

"Every transfer refers to something stable which is not transferred. A delusion can be defined only in terms of a nondelusion. Thus, what is suspect always refers to the non-suspect." Even if God, therefore, is but an idol, that is, the product or sole justification of one's mystification, it does not follow—far from it—that one's relation to the idol does not transcend the idol. Which means, on another level, that there is no experience of the human reality by which this reality can be reduced. Likewise, God can be reduced to an idol. But no idol can reduce God. There is, and there is not, a difference between God and the idol.

And if it should be asked why God should always appear as an idol, or the "non-suspect . . . in the midst of suspect things," the answer might very well lie in the fact that "what has been defined, explained, and interpreted is only an expression of the unique phenomenon which underlies whatever is explicable, definable, and interpretable." Which amounts to saying that at the root of every phenomenon of culture there is a consciousness which is "irreplaceable" and whose appearance can but be "derisory." Cheating or committing a fraud is the price either for raising or for not raising the question of God. Faith can only be bad faith. On this, believer and unbeliever are agreed. And all the arguments for the existence of God cannot turn idolatry into faith. "The believer," Durandeaux writes, "exists only to the degree that he questions. The believer does not exist only because he cannot exist complacently." Or, "my practices can be religious only because they are not religious."

God, in other words, is not as we imagine him. Or, rather, he is other than the product of our imagination. Now, Durandeaux points out with great subtlety, that if "this concept I have of God is also the product of the civilization that formed me," it follows "I will recognize God only if the testimony I accept fits the mold my civilization has given me." There should be, in other words, continuity between "God" and civilization, or between revelation and culture.

But what kind of continuity can there be if it does not also witness to a concomitant discontinuity? In that case, is fideism the only alternative as far as the believer is concerned? *No* would be Durandeaux's answer; by not so strange a coincidence he here finds himself in partial agreement with those who precisely try to reduce revelation to culture. For him, however, culture could not reduce revelation, unless by doing so it also "revealed" the presence of something which is neither reduced nor reducible. Whether believers or unbelievers, we are like "most Jews [who] did not recognize Jesus of Nazareth because he did not correspond to their concept of God." Did he even correspond to the idea they had of man? More appropriately, does man today correspond wholly to our reductionist idea of man? Or does he transcend it at the same time? Indeed, what ultimately cultural reductionism fails to reduce is man himself—man whose question can never be so formulated as automatically either to validate or to invalidate the question of God.

One must admire Jacques Durandeaux's candor and, at the same time, not overlook the rigor of his argument: it forces him to acknowledge that atheism cannot be seriously dealt with if theism is not by the same token abandoned. It also forces him to admit that if absolute theism can only lead to absolute atheism, the believer may not surreptitiously settle for some kind of mitigated or relative theism. Nor can the unbeliever, on the other hand, rest his case on an atheism which, by being itself also the product of his cultural situation, would in turn become merely the expression of a new absolutism. In any event, Durandeaux's concern lies with that aspect of the problem which involves the believer, as was Kierkegaard's when he said, God does not exist, he is. Durandeaux goes even further.

Indeed, saying that God is but does not exist may well just be an ultimate attempt not to acknowledge the death of God and, instead, to seek refuge in some Pascalian notion of God still "sensible to the heart" if no longer otherwise tangible. Whether "up there," "out there," or "deep down," all these notions of God's being cannot conceal the hiatus that yawns between a faith, which cannot adequately understand itself without bodying forth into a culture, and a culture which has neutralized that faith. Thinking of God as a being or thinking of him as Being, neither way removes the supernaturalist scaffolding which now indefectibly gives theism away. Nor does giving up theism guarantee that one has in fact removed all scaffolding or, simply, that one has thrown away all crutches. Giving up the image of a supernatural God does not necessarily mean that the problematics of our time has been duly taken into consideration.

If no question can be exported out of its own problematics, since the question which corresponds to it would thereby lose its meaning, one must be careful, however, not to adjudicate our present problematics by means of categories that have survived their own. The classical problematics of the Christian era consisted in a debate on the relation between faith and reason. More precisely it led to the question whether one can

demonstrate the existence of a God in whom one already believes. Our present problematics is radically different. It arises
from the consciousness that whatever God is, he is also a projection of one's own image. And the question to which this
leads is, "Can I assert the existence of a being whose image I
myself have created?"

A radical shift, if not a caesura, has occurred between the
two questions. The first concerns the being of God, hidden
behind that which is, as the source and origin of all that is.
It is focused on the concept of *archè* (or its corollary *telos*),
and presupposes therefore that the world, having a beginning
and an end, is *ipso facto* meaningful *per se*. Classical metaphysics rests on this assumption, and that is why, once the
latter question is invalidated, history still remaining the privi-
leged arena of God's deeds, becomes the chief concept of the
believer's self-understanding. And one kind of absolutism is
replaced by another. There is no point in freeing oneself from
the past if one is to be riveted to a no less inescapable future.

But, according to biblical thought, God is not so much *archè*
or *telos* as he is the *eschaton,* namely, that which history cannot reduce nor the world produce; that which is here and
through which, here and now, the world is offered to man's
freedom and his responsibility. That is why, I suspect, Durandeaux does not bother whether God *is* but whether God *is
here.* Faith has nothing to do with a God who simply would
be, who simply *is,* if, first and foremost, he were not also *here.*
The question which confronts faith today is not whether God
is, but whether he *is here.* It is not a question of God's being
but of his *Dasein,* his being-there in the world. Without the
world God is not, just as without worshippers God is not.

The world is the arena of God's irruption into worldliness, of God's tangibility.

It is no wonder, then, that the grace of God, as the tradition itself had it, cannot be found except where we expect it least —in the world. Indeed, only if God is the *eschaton* and not merely some metaphysical *archè,* nor the supreme being, nor the *telos,* can the things of this world be asserted for their own sake, even though theirs is a maimed or, as on the cross, tragically muted eloquence of God's reality. Could there be, indeed, any other stumbling block than the product of man's imagination, than the object of one's credulousness—or its rationalization into one's incapacity to believe?

So many stupidities have been voiced and so many have, in spite of oneself, been heard about the death of God, that Jacques Durandeaux's austerely ironic and maieutic book, *Living Questions to Dead Gods,* will render caducous many similar disquisitions and divagations upon the same theme. Short as it is, here is a book which, the more one wrestles with it, the more fascinating it becomes. Its simplicity has the deceptive nakedness of truth. And its irony is not that of causticity but that of charity. That is why with Durandeaux the death of God never becomes a shibboleth. It signifies a cultural phenomenon and marks the transition from a certain view of the world to one that is so radically different that they seem to be, if in fact they are not, mutually exclusive.

Different authors have used different terms to describe this transition from a supernaturalistic view of the world to a so-called objective one which contents itself with viewing the world as it is. And what distinguishes the two world views has been stated by means of various dualities designed to express a certain fundamental irreconcilability between them.

Let us remind ourselves of some of these dualities. For example, the classical Christian conception of the world, Bultmann says, is mythological and stands in sharp antithesis to our present scientific conception. Or it is said that the former is transcendental, the latter, immanental. Elsewhere, the first is seen as the conveyor of the sacred whereas the second is totally absorbed in the profane. Likewise, it is claimed that today it is not the religious but the secular which is the vector of our self-understanding. As I have tried to show elsewhere, this transition itself is indicative of an irreversible leveling-down in the light of which no hope is left of recovering the meaning of lost symbols—a statement which does not mean that Christianity has no future but that its future does not depend upon, nor does it necessitate, any recovery of lost symbols. Or else this would imply that the truth of Christianity stands or falls with a given view of the world.

What, therefore, has erroneously been interpreted as pessimism results not only from a realistic assessment of the uniqueness of our own historical situation but also from an intellectually sobered-up allegiance to the Christian faith. The Gospel was never meant to mediate a mere world view, even if it can neither be proclaimed nor heard except through a given view of the world—and that can only be one's own. This indeed was the case throughout the Christian era itself. The difference is that today's situation stems from the fact that the desacralization of the world and the secularization of Christianity, both of which had been concomitantly taking place ever since Christianity became a cultural factor first in the Mediterranean and then in the Western world, have brought about a mutation of our *Lebenswelt,* a mutation whose significance is not properly or adequately assessed if it is explained only in terms of a mere transition. For what has occurred between a cultural epoch which, for all practical purposes, embodies the Christian faith and one which rests on its expropriation, or its secularization, is nothing other than a mutation.

The "death of God" as the expression of this cultural phenomenon is the term which for better or for worse has been used to describe and account for what, at different moments, points to this mutation of our traditional ways of understanding the experience of the human reality and its world. Politically, economically, socially, as well as ethically and scientifically what the West has witnessed is a switch from the theistic assumptions that operated in these various fields to a methodology which is basically atheistic: that is, it forbids us to take God for granted or simply to begin any kind of inquiry with a God-hypothesis. And this not only can but also must apply to religion, to theology.

Such also is basically the framework of Durandeaux's meditation. And I can only praise him for the restraint with which he makes us conscious of it. He hardly uses the phrase "death of God," but speaks instead of the fundamental incompatibility between what he terms the classical and the contemporary problematics, and contents himself with attributing the reasons for this radical change to Marx, Freud, and Einstein. Not that they are responsible for the death of God. But the views they expressed only endorsed a *fait accompli,* even if it is only recently that theology has been able to come to grips with it. This is not to suggest that Durandeaux unreservedly agrees with the contention that the religious view of man is but a concealment of man's alienation or the justification of some neurotic obsession or the intellectual diet for a hypertrophied view of the world. But certainly the thought alone that religious attitudes can thus be reduced needs and calls for careful consideration. After all, "our problem is not whether one can succeed, without divine grace, in demonstrating the existence of God to other believers and the Church," as was the case according to the medieval conception of reality.

We live in a different world, and if faith still must be lived in our world, it cannot be except "as something other than obstinacy, as something other than an attachment to traditions designed to ward off the perils of a new world, as something other than a refuge or a watchful fear of terrible forces and the torment of eternal suffering." The world in which we live revolves around a completely different question, and "this new question reflects the fact of our living in a historical context which has become consciously post-Marxian and post-Freudian; it assumes that we have accepted the validity of a series of criticisms, and analyses of certain aspects of our religious practices and that our problem is one of discovering how we can conduct a religious endeavor which is valid *in the philosopher's eyes.*"

These last words are underlined by Durandeaux himself who, I think, does not mean that faith must be accommodated to whatever the philosophical fancy of the moment happens to be, but that it must be homogeneous with the world view in terms of which even the believer must understand his faith. "We must emphasize that nothing is given, that everything is constructed, including the religious practice. The discussion tends either to build up the practice or to destroy it. The believer has created the philosopher, and the philosopher has created the believer. The religious man's discourse creates God, and God creates him with his living discourse. If there is an absolute reality, it can only be the goal of our discussion, not its starting point. If I am a believer, it is God toward whom my words are moving. I attain freedom by recognizing myself as a cultural product and refusing to be satisfied. My discourse, the examination of my discourse, and the analysis of this examination lead to my ultimate freedom. And this is also the process whereby I find I am both a philosopher and a believer."

What I discover then unveils nothing but the application, a further implication, of the New Testament's definition of the believer as one who can but confess his unbelief. Faith, in other words, is not what segregates the believer from the unbeliever. For such segregation would amount to claiming either that revelation is a cultural datum or that it cannot be conjoined with culture. In the first case, it would be reduced to a dimension of culture. In the second, it would contradict the classical contention that God is a God who acts through history and that, correspondingly, there can be no Christian faith which would be divested of all cultural obligation. This would also contradict what the Church has been throughout the ages (more or less appropriately, of course), namely, among other things to be sure, the Christian way of constructing the world and society.

But what can Church mean today if the world can no longer be construed as it used to be? Indeed, yesterday's world was one which "gave meaning to certain problems, for example, discussions on the demonstrability of the existence of God. But the meaning of these problems was secreted by yesterday's world—a world which was well-defined, namely, the West with its Christian culture which was dominated by Roman Catholic dogmatics. The world has changed, as have the problems, and the meaning given these problems is merely counterfeit species in a new and different world." It is no surprise, then, if religion no longer is, as Tillich said, the substance of culture: the Church itself does not correspond to our world, but merely prolongs one that precisely our world has survived.

What, then, are we left with if neither our conceptions of God nor our understanding of the Church can withstand the rise and fall of cultures? Are we left with mere relativism? In avowing the death of God, Durandeaux writes, all I have done is to win emancipation from "an absolute which was merely a product. Would I dare to make the claim that I myself have discovered myself? No, for this would mean considering myself free from all mythmaking; it would mean secretly introducing the absolute which I have rid myself of. No, here I am, poor, helpless, existing by chance in this time and place, surrounded by other men. And we have a world to build. Setting up the absolute is not within my powers. I am asked, 'What are you doing to your faith, to the Church, to Jesus Christ.' To this I reply that I broach only those questions Jesus Christ puts to me, in other words, broach only those questions which I cannot ask myself. The Churches bring people together who take these questions seriously, and this is what faith represents first and foremost—these communities, these gatherings of people who consider the questions Christ raises a serious matter."

Indeed, is faith or the experience of authentic existence

anything but what "cannot be expressed without having to be denied," what cannot "be denied without having to be expressed"?

If faith has any future, it will have to be neither Catholic nor Protestant. And it will not be Christian unless it has ceased to be ecclesiastical. For the world is the arena of faith —not the Church. Nor will theology be Christian if it continues to preserve a confessional rather than an essentially ecumenical character. Much less can it, in view of the present methodological atheism which governs our understanding of the world, retain even the apologetic flavor it so liberally or rather so self-satisfiedly exhaled in the face of unbelief. Today's problematics annuls both confessional and polemical theology, and no theologizing can occur that ignores this. The first and most urgent thing to be done is, therefore, to take stock of what roots one can and must grow, not of what ancestry theology can claim for itself.

Faith is not a matter of pedigree. It is a way of being implanted in the world, not transplanted into it. The world has no meaning in itself. And what alone can give meaning to it is both congruous and incongruous with it. Define the term as you will, it is faith alone which can overcome the world and accept it. Faith, however, is not some kind of an absurd leap out of one's congruence with the world. For the leap into faith is absurd only because, although it should be necessitated by the experience of the human reality, it is not. Faith, indeed, is both congruous and incongruous with the world, for the world is the only place where one lives by faith, not because one ought to but because one can.

In all these respects Jacques Durandeaux's exacting meditation is of the kind that helps bring to maturity a much needed and long-delayed reflection on faith which takes into account the cleavage so threatening between Christianity and the world. But while hastening this process of maturation, Durandeaux's intellectual grace shuns all facile argumentation and excels in not leaving unturned any stone which must be turned. Indeed, he deserves to make his own Kierkegaard's statement that he may have made the task of becoming a Christian so difficult as to prevent any increase in the number of those who are Christian by descent. But Durandeaux's argument is as simple as it is clearly cogent and exigent.

Saint Paul argued that in order to become a Christian no convert from paganism need first assume Judaism, that particular religious heritage which precisely could not accept Jesus as the Christ and for which God was therefore dead. Like St. Paul, Durandeaux makes the point that there is no other intellectual sacrifice that must be made than that one alone which, because it is antithetical to faith, is also antithetical to the problematics itself in terms of which faith is to be thought and lived. That sacrifice is, as it was also in Paul's day, the sacrifice of a certain religious conceptuality which mistakes ancestry for authentic faith and, reducing God to his image, makes him into an idol. Moreover, Durandeaux leads us to remark that it is no longer a question whether God is this or that, *aliter* or *taliter*; the question is: How can one break through the circle of being produced by those very images one has produced?

Clearly, then, saying that God is a cultural product does not invalidate faith. As a matter of fact, what Durandeaux skillfully shows is this: whatever God is he must be conceptualized. That is to say, God is both "tangible" and Wholly Other. While the tangibility is best attested to by the Catholic tradition, it is the Protestant tradition which best witnesses to the Otherness. But it goes without saying that the tangibility is best expressed in and through the Otherness, and vice versa.

I am not suggesting that Durandeaux's book is a theological treatise: his aim is to clarify the grounds upon which theological reflection can take place. And, to say the least, the lucidity of his argument is compelling. It is compelling, because in particular of the power with which he convinces us that if the death of God separates us at all from traditional theism, there is no alternative but to abandon the dogmatic conceptuality of the past, and to be bold enough to reject it in its entirety. The reason is very simple, and it cannot be both upheld and spared: "Therefore, if we aspire to thoroughness and precision, we must hold to the idea that every question has its problematics and must be considered within it and *cannot be transposed into another one.* Any given question has a corresponding problematics which we should track down; if the problematics has changed, the question has lost its meaning. Then, the question the philosopher asks today . . . should be, 'What are the conditions which will make for serious religious practices, free from all mystification?' " That traditional believers will be frightened by such an approach scarcely needs to be observed. They have, however, nothing to lose but a dead God.

But they might also learn that what the Christ-event shows is precisely that God is not exhausted by our ideas, our concepts, or our images of him. So that, with or without them, the task is to live without being reduced by them. And such a task, beyond the apparent antinomy of belief and unbelief, can only be assumed by faith, that is, by what is ultimately both original and irreducible, an echoing of God's irruption into the world. Not that Durandeaux at this point reintroduces the picture of a "God beyond God," of a God beyond our inadequate images of him. For God is what corresponds to that which even these worn-out images cannot ultimately reduce. Indeed, the world itself is what prevents the objectification of God—or else God would be a datum of the universe.

The world, one might therefore say, is the "objective" dimension of God's reality, and this dimension remains objective only to the extent that the reality of God is not objectified. The truth of faith is not a truth among other truths, though it is not encountered without these truths. As Durandeaux puts it, "Either my affirmation that God is there is suggested to me by material in my culture, in which case there is no true irruption, or my affirmation already contains *something more* than what my cultural environment has led me to adopt." And since culture and world are somewhat synonymous, what, as far as I understand it, Durandeaux's alternative drives home is the notion that the reality of God is given *with* the world: it can be grasped only through the world, but only if the world is not fraudulently hypostatized; if the world, instead of being a given by which man is determined, is what man must construct. "Man," as Durandeaux says, "finds himself the creator where he once thought of himself as the created." And this is an idea which, indeed, coincides with the biblical myth of creation.

To say that the world is created not only means that it does not of itself constitute an harmonious whole, a self-contained cosmos. It also means that it does not determine itself, let alone man's action. It only is what comes about between God and man. To use biblical language, it is what happens when God speaks. It is God's "speech." And for that reason, it is not extraneous to God's reality, although it cannot be identified with God.

Is not speech, indeed, what prohibits any identification between what is said and what is done? And is not the deed what speaks louder than words—than those words of ours which may deny God even while our deeds frustrate them of their denials. For what are these but an avowal of our words' impotence to speak the word? As Rilke put it in one of his French poems:

> ... le chant des eaux
> n'est qu'un excès de silence,
> de ce silence entre les mots
> qui, en rythmes, avancent.
> (Werke, p. 568)

Or to quote Durandeaux: "This affirmative reply [to God's question] alone enables the believer to speak of his experience [of God]." For what could be an experience which was itself determined by one's environment? Hence, there can be experience only when experience is not "a new human product," when "this experience can only result from an irruption of God, recognized now through the believer's adherence."

But if on the other hand, it seems that "God keeps silent, [it is] perhaps. . . .[because] he is absent, . . . he does not exist"; or is it perhaps because "it is clear that recourse to this

experience is not enough to allow a person to state his position
to others. The experience can be authenticated by God alone;
God alone can put the question of God to man in a serious
manner." Even the experience of God's reality is not one
which presupposes a certain lack through which to assert God
in the phenomenon of consciousness. For God cannot be ex-
pected—he is not a want: the world indeed suffices in full-
filling the exercise of man's creativity and can even make God
quite superflous.

What, then, does Durandeaux mean by the phrase "the
irruption of God," especially if God is, moreover, a "legend"
of my cultural milieu? Mindful of the obstacle, Durandeaux
puts his skill in the suggestion that precisely "God's irruption,"
that is, his irreducible presentness to the world, is meaningful only if it is not presupposed by the world. Is this not, also,
what he actually means when he admits rather unexpectedly
that to ask whether God exists is to cheat, if only because it
would presuppose a certain idea of God in my head? And if
so, either I would be merely wondering whether some real
God corresponds to what I have in mind, corresponds to my
culturally-determined image of a God, or, under such circumstances, no question of God could today be a serious question.

Small wonder, then, that Durandeaux states with tongue in
cheek, or, if you will, with an irrepressible amount of Kierke-
gaardian irony, "In short, the question of God is serious only
if it is formulated by someone other than myself. Either the
concept of God is a product of myself and of the human environment of my life, and I question its seriousness, or this
question is put to me by God himself, and we have found the

one and only condition for the seriousness of the question. All else is chimera. The problem is to learn whether this question is mine or the Other's; this, and this alone, determines whether the question can be reduced." That is to say, in order to speak about God nothing else is available but the instrumentality of human speech—but man cannot speak about God for to do so would necessitate that he cease to be human at the same time.

Are we then brought back once again to the classical notion of the ineffability of God? It would seem so, but with this difference, however, that for the classics God's ineffability corresponds to man's inadequacy, whereas, for Durandeaux, it is a man's capacity for speech that makes God ineffable. He writes, "The paradox of the ineffable is that it is expressed and that if it were not expressed, ineffability would not exist. By the same token, the experience of God is the paradox of paradoxes—one finds it absolutely necessary to keep silent while experiencing an absolute necessity to speak."

Silence thus is to speech as God is to the world and to man. And if speech is but an excess of silence, the world is but an excess of God's creativity, the instrument of his presentness to man. Far from God's hedging in either man or the world, through God the world can be invented instead of inventoried, and man can, instead of suffering destiny, invent it.

GABRIEL VAHANIAN

FOREWORD

Is there a problem of God?

Are the questions alive—or are they dead? Such an introduction may suggest that our inquiry is adopting the perspective of disbelief. These pages are a plea on behalf of disbelievers. We can understand their needs and the meaning of their aspirations only if we grasp the total picture of their experience and conduct. We must speak of *disbelievers* in the plural, for this experience is shared by a whole new world of men.

Who are these disbelievers? Skeptical philosophers indicting the religious practices of believers? Believers who have been "demythologized," who confront other believers who have not been "demythologized"? People who no longer believe, but who confront those who do? Or, those who appear to believe for the wrong reasons in opposition to those who think they believe properly? Actually, all of these types are disbelievers—and all of them may be present in each of us. I hope that a good number of people will recognize themselves in this picture. I suspect that they will.

Is there authenticity in disbelief? In fact, is not disbelief a more secure path precisely because it is stricter and more demanding? In the end, will not disbelievers turn out to be far more serious than we had thought?

The structure of this work

I began this book with some thoughts that are closest to my heart and constitute the core of what I wanted to say. I put them down as succinctly as possible, writing spontaneously and using the first words that came into my head. I was later forced to recognize that these words are very ambiguous.

Next, I reflected on this text, taking each proposition or group of propositions in turn. This first reaction is designed as a commentary and is the second section of the book.

The next step was to explore what further meaning there might be in the first spontaneous text and the commentary. I wished to see if my reflections had any deeper meaning which had earlier escaped me. This forms the third portion of the book.

I
Prose Poem of a Kind

I am almost sure that God is there.
God is a very serious question;
I suspect his presence.
But no discussion of God is satisfactory,
and religious practices are almost always suspect.
One might even say they are *always* suspect.
The criticisms of Marx and Freud are sound.

So how am I to survive?
If coherent criticism makes everything come unglued,
my only real security will come from sticking to my deepest convictions—in other words, from following my conscience.
My conscience may be somewhat uncertain, but for
lack of anything better, it is the most
trustworthy source of guidance I can find.

So I find I am both a philosopher and a believer:
a philosopher, because I am always on guard
against myself as a believer;
a believer, because the Christian message
concerns and challenges me personally.

31

My religious life is formed by this two-sided tension.
   The believer in me defies the philosopher,
      and the philosopher never succeeds in silencing
      the believer.
   This is the dialectic I am striving to analyze
      because this dialectic is the essence of my reli-
      gious experience.

How is such a dialogue possible? What foundation does
   it have?
First, this dialogue presupposes that both men are worthy
participants:
   the *philosopher* accepts the *believer* as a worthy partner, in
      spite of everything, including Marx and Freud;
   the *believer* accepts the *philosopher* as a worthy partner, in
      spite of all the condemnations over the centuries.

And this in turn presupposes that this dialogue is a source
of life,
   that it is the necessary condition for religious progress;
   that it essentially characterizes religious progress;
   that it is identical with my religious life,
because it enables me to approach God.

II

Initial Reflection on
the Prose Poem

I am almost sure that God is there.

Let us begin by discussing what the category 1 "almost sure" means.* Being "sure" that God *is there* would mean saying that God *is there* in the same way that a table *is there.* At this point, I cannot state that his presence and the table's presence can be thought of in the same way. But neither can I state that God is not there. Now although this last remark stresses what I *cannot* say, it contains an affirmation: I cannot deny or get rid of God without feeling a certain *resistance.* This resistance reveals that the affirmation of God contains elements that have a hold on me. Basically, however, what I am holding on to is not God but something I have myself added. For my affirmation of God to be valid at the stage I have now reached, it would have to be totally "disinterested," to the point that it no longer concerned me whether or not God existed.

Since the question of God is directly related to my ultimate fate, I would have to be prepared to accept death at any time and to be without fear of any possible retribution. In my

* All the footnotes are on pages 154-160.

imagination these two requirements may seem possible; that is, I can imagine myself actually accepting the fact of death and fearing nothing that God might visit upon me. But there is a difficulty: can I be sure that to accept these two requirements in my imagination means that I am really doing so? Perhaps I would always have to doubt my own sincerity.

This quasi-certainty is an insoluble problem and probably a false problem in any case. Analyzing it, however, reinforces my grasp of the need for disinterestedness in dealing with the problem of God. It also makes me realize that the dry coldness of theological discourse, which results from this kind of disinterestedness, is a relative guarantee of the effort to escape from the suspect elements in our statements about God.

In the statement "I am almost sure," the "I am" is just as difficult to deal with as the "almost sure." The two are closely related, since the "almost sure" throws me back upon the subject—myself—to make me accept the impossible supposition that I could be settled stably in this kind of quasi-certitude.

This brings us to the clause "God is there." The problem is to discover just what these words can mean. They can have no meaning beyond the content I put into them when I speak. This content is not only mine; it belongs to a whole culture. In other words, my statement "God is there" is mine because of the culture that formed me. My ultimate affirmation that "God is there" is suspect because it presupposes a meaning bearing the stamp of a particular cultural mold. For me to affirm God, he must be a totally irruptive presence. But I must agree that in order to name this irruptive presence I have to start from my own expectations and those of the culture that formed me. This God would be an irruptive presence that answers some trend of my culture, or else a presence created by the meeting of a new element with my expectations. This is double jeopardy: some may be seeking God, yet not recognize him; others not seeking him may have no notion what to name him. This is the double jeopardy God himself faces, if he breaks into man's world: to be either the *Rejected* or the *Unexpected*. This was the problem of Jesus of Nazareth in his dialogue with both Jews and Gentiles.

The statement "God is there" means that I have recognized an irruption and I suspect whose presence this may be.

God is a very serious question.

What does the word "question" mean when we use it about God?

First of all, it indicates a state of incompleteness: if I had met and recognized God and had entered an absolute and definitive union with him, God could no longer be a "question." This incompleteness is a result of my advancing toward a hypothesis that my cultural environment suggests to me. The question means that we are discussing a possible presence, neither attained nor dismissed; it means both the absence of a presence and the presence of an absence. Why then qualify such a "question" as "very serious"?

Undoubtedly because I cannot completely resolve it. I can explain the images of God which I or my culture formulate: the God of alienation, the God produced by our own psychic projections, the God who is the "garbage heap of our dreams" (Jean Rostand). But how am I to explain a God who might surprise me, a God I am not expecting, a God whom I do not seriously know, an unpredictable, not-absurd God?

Of course, even an unpredictable God has already been anticipated—but only as existing and not in terms of an image. I can strip all these images from my expectations, but then what are these expectations without images? Expectations without images belong on the level of accomplishment and fulfillment. But I experience my own contingency as incompleteness; because I am autonomous in my being, I aspire to necessary existence. Is not my existential experience as a contingent being the main basis for the question of God?

The question is "serious" because it touches the very core of my being and concerns me to the most intense degree possible. What is serious must concern me intensely, or else it is not really serious. This being so, is not the "serious" what affects *me* most? But this kind of "seriousness" is not necessarily truly serious. It also will be suspect. Is there no other kind of seriousness besides the seriousness of everything that touches my existence and the seriousness of whatever concerns my existence as a contingent being?

But can there be a discussion which does not affect me? Would a "disinterested" discussion be human? In this sense, any discussion in which man is the issue will affect me deeply. I may be affected because the discussion concerns my frustrations; this is the level of passions and motivations. I may be affected because of my concept of my destiny and my position in the universe as a contingent being; here also we deal in frustrations, passions, and motivations, but the approach is different.

Why is my attitude different in the second sense? It is different because I am able to contemplate and accept my own death. If I think of death as something I reject and revolt against, even in the most personal way possible, I will be affected in the first sense. If I think of my death as an eventual fact, as something on the horizon and integrated into my life, if I am neither obsessed by death nor in revolt against it, I will be able to imagine a world where one is not obliged to die, and I will, therefore, be affected only in the second sense.

This "disinterestedness" seems my best safeguard in this endeavor. My need for God frightens me, for my need is part of me and God is the absolutely Other. I try to become involved in dialogue with the Other in a "disinterested" manner. This is probably the best safeguard against encountering myself under the guise of the Other. If God is not truly this Other, he is not God. I would also say as much for human beings: if I do not consider another individual as truly "other," then he is not a person to me. The Other is not anticipated. In childhood one is caught up with himself. But becoming an adult means encountering the Other—this presence we cannot anticipate—and loving him.

Therefore, if I feel myself affected by the question of God, it is probably because this God who affects me is still myself or several fragments of myself. But if the question of God no longer affected me, would I still want to explore it? Perhaps not. Let me suggest that for it to be really possible for this question no longer to affect me, then God can only appear as an irruptive presence in my world, a world where there had been no question of him. Some have interpreted Pascal in terms of superficial phychologism. They maintain that he sees God coming simply to fill a lack we feel as anxiety. If this is all Pascal had to say, his thought did not amount to very much. But unquestionably he meant something quite different.

I am now in a difficult position, for it seems that there are two ways in which I can be affected, one of which makes my discussion suspect, while the other does not destroy its validity. Have I drawn the distinction between them clearly enough? I would say yes if we are speaking of what we experience; but in terms of theoretical analysis I still have my doubts.

After saying that the question of God is serious, I must now go on to say that its seriousness does not arise simply because it is being asked. Its seriousness requires conditions I had not envisaged in my spontaneous formulation. I must now conclude that the question of God can be a serious one in light of certain conditions which I will attempt to define in the remaining part of my commentary. I suspect that these conditions will be rigorous, calling for thoroughness and precision, for I now realize that God is an irruptive presence in my world, a world where the question of God no longer exists. If my question is to be "serious," I must reconcile it with this irruptive initiative of God. I will deal with this in later pages. I find that what I mistakenly considered serious in the beginning may not be so serious after all, and that it is important at this point to discover what conditions will make the question of God serious. I have already mentioned a disinterested approach to the question, and I suspect that another condition will come to light when we consider how the question originated.

I suspect his presence.

What does it mean to "have one's suspicions" about something? Are we speaking of the kind of "impression" we get when we are reading and we suddenly feel that we are being watched? What I mean by "having a suspicion" is similar to this sensation, but added to it is the notion of *imperceptibility*. Imperceptible does not mean not perceivable; rather it designates a perception which is near the threshold of perceptibility. There are echoes here of the passage in the Bible (1 Kings 19: 9-13) where Elijah does not find God in the hurricane, the earthquake, or in the fire: God's passing is signified by a gentle breeze.

Sign, indication, interpretation, and *inquiry* are ideas bound up with the notion of "suspicion." If I "have my suspicions," I have discovered a sign of something I am seeking. And this means that I am conducting some kind of deliberate or unconscious inquiry: deliberate when I suspect a particular person of a crime, for example; unconscious or virtual when I suspect that someone may be in a house that ought to be empty. In the second case I am not actively looking for anyone, but someone's presence is nevertheless an object of inquiry to the degree that it is conceivable and possible that somebody may be present.

The idea of "suspicion" means that a reality is revealed to me through signs which I am able to perceive. This implies some kind of materialization and the establishment, between the suspected reality and myself, of a common denominator which allows me to begin to grow familiar with this reality.

Once again my own initiative is called for in my recognition of God's irruption into my life. Having suspicions about God's presence brings me face to face with a *personal* question and inquiry.

Suspicion is an introduction to reasoning. To have suspicions means to begin searching in the appearances of meaning for the meaning of the appearances. Suspicion puts me on the alert. The time when I was in serene possession of ideas, certainties, and things draws to a close. Why? My suspicion is the child of my needs and dissatisfaction; it requires light and it complains at darkness. In short, it is the child of both darkness and light, born in an intermediary region where a striving for order and meaning begins. I suspect because my hypothesis of meaning is so fruitful that it surpasses the apparent meaninglessness around me. Or, it may happen that the accumulated ill effects of living with meaninglessness may arouse within me demands for exactness. Through order I awaken to space, through rhythm I awaken to time. And so the world develops in my image. My reason finds its proper path because it believes in a continuity of being, a proportionality of all things. My suspicions arise because of an attack on the conviction that harmony among all beings is possible and because of a confused perception of the complicity of all existents. To suspect is to begin to reason, to be born to meaning.

But no discussion of God is satisfactory.

Only God could give a suitable account of himself. Only he could deliver the "total" discourse about himself. Even a perfect human discourse about God would be incomplete at best, and could never do full justice to God's reality.

Therefore, if man is always in the foreground of his discussions about God, what value do those discussions have? Man inevitably projects himself into everything he says and does; his observations on extrinsic reality are always full of himself, colored by himself, patterned after his own nature, expressed within the limits of his style. Man's discussion of God invariably speaks of all the aspects of his own condition, whether the author is Paul or Augustine, Gregory of Nyssa or Bernard of Clairvaux, Francis de Sales or John Henry Newman.

Because I am aware of this fact and because sciences of man illustrate it with profound insight, no discussion of God can really satisfy me. But what would a truly satisfying discourse be like?

First, it would have to be complete. Every human element of the speaker would have to be eliminated so that God, the subject of the discourse, would be the only one to speak. Second, it would have to be in my language, completely *understandable* to me in every sense of the word. The satisfaction would result from the fulfillment of my entire self, of all my potentialities, as I listened to the discourse. This satisfaction would be the fruit of this completeness.

This is why all human discussion of God can only be unsatisfactory to the listener. He ought to reject such discourses. Whatever satisfaction we experience from them is in our imagination.

And religious practices are almost always suspect.

It is the *satisfying* side of religious practices that should put us on our guard. Practices which answer a personal need refer to the nature of the need and nothing more.

But the individual who is practicing religion often does not really know what his need is. The seriousness of the question, however, cannot admit such ambiguity. Traditional thought has scarcely touched on the question of the clearly unformulated needs of the religious person. This is what the Marxists and Freudians criticize. Once these needs are formulated, the individual is turned back into himself just as he is about to lose himself in the object of his need. When he has identified this object as the answer to a hidden need, he finally recognizes it as himself mirrored in his own discourse. True progress begins only when the follower of ostensibly religious practices is forced to confront himself and accept himself as he is: a naked cheat, guilty of a falsehood which he may well repeat unless he continues to recognize the need-response mechanism of his religious practices.

Religious practices will always be suspect until we manage to integrate our needs into the asceticism of "the spiritual life." Even the most serious, most demanding period of human life is not able to raise our practices completely above suspicion. But accepting ourselves as suspect is a decisive step forward. Since the terms of religious practices are beyond the scope of science, there are only two solutions: we can refuse to recognize, and indeed we can reject, the idea that we are suspect, or else we can accept it.

One might even say they are always suspect.

Is it possible to think of religious practices that are not suspect? If I analyze them, will I occasionally find even one that is clearly beyond suspicion? The answer is no. The lives of the mystics themselves raise extremely difficult questions. But we are led to the idea that a given practice, however suspect it may be—in other words, despite whatever suspicions it may arouse in us—may be, at the same time and without alteration of its content, meaningful in a non-suspect way. The non-suspect does not necessarily lie on this side of the suspect or on the far side of it; they are mixed together. This is an important paradox. A particular religious practice may indicate alienation and yet have some other authentic meaning at the same time. Therefore, what seems suspect always seems beyond suspicion at the same time.

We can postulate, then, that the non-suspect is present within the suspect. But an alienated habit necessarily refers to some radical motivation which is its source. Every transfer refers to something stable which is not transferred. A delusion can be defined only in terms of a non-delusion. Thus, what is suspect always refers to the non-suspect. But why is what is non-suspect always found in the midst of suspect things?

Non-suspect practices belong in the realm of some original, purely hypothetical innocence. Contact with evil creates suspicion. A world of exclusively non-suspect practices would suppose that our motives could no longer lead to evil and that past evil had not marked us in any way. It would mean that the structure of the world we are placed in is entirely good, that it does not deform us in any way or blind us to anything.

The criticisms of Marx and Freud are sound.

What does this mean?

A certain debunking of religious practices has succeeded. A good number of ostensibly "religious" responses have been shown to be other than they were thought to be. The religious realities to which they were supposed to correspond turned out to be not specifically religious.

This statement presupposes that we accept the Marxist and Freudian criticism of religious practices; it implies that Marx and Freud were successful in their criticism of certain aspects of religious practices. If religious practices are no more than what Marx and Freud maintain they are, then they have been explained away. But is there possibly something more to them? This is what we must consider. As long as they are *merely* what Marx and Freud claim, the matter is settled; indeed, it is settled to whatever degree they are what these men say they are.

Marx described religion as alienation and Freud considered it as neurotic; my remark does not challenge these views, and we are not about to go back over the theories in question. There was a time in the history of Western civilization when it was fruitful to criticize the Marxian and Freudian criticisms of religious practices. We are beyond that point now. Our present purpose is this: bearing in mind the Marxian and Freudian analyses, we must ask ourselves whether sound religious practices are not possible despite them. This question we may approach from two directions: first, in terms of the debunked religious practices themselves; second, in terms of the possibility that there are religious practices which Marx and Freud have not explained away.

It is not possible that the religious practices successfully explained away by Marx and Freud (and we consider that those they dealt with are in fact explained away once and for all) contain elements which were not analyzed by Marx and Freud, elements which have not been and cannot be dismissed? In other words, within alienated or neurotic religious practices may there not be something that Marx and Freud did not perceive? Or to put it another way, is it not possible that these practices also contain an attitude which does not fall into the category of alienation or neurosis? Is an alienated or neurotic religious attitude totally explained once we have labeled it as such? Marx and Freud claimed that such practices were meaningless in religious terms. They maintain that what had been generally considered religiously *significant* is actually not meaningful in those terms.

Our remarks take this for granted. But may not certain elements which did not enter into their investigations remain significant? *This does not mean that we find the analyses of Marx and Freud insufficient,* for we can consider their work sound as far as it goes. It means instead that religious practices could reside in a different order of meaning, on a level that does not admit, and perhaps necessarily escapes, this kind of analytic process. Our idea is that some elements have been rightly dismissed but that there may be others which have been left intact.

The other possibility is that certain religious practices may *totally* escape the Marxist and Freudian analyses. Is this a real possibility in view of our already having concluded that religious practices are always ambiguous and, therefore, always suspect?

The interpretive sciences can examine and satisfactorily describe the nature of human behavior; but precisely because their function is to *interpret,* their findings cannot be considered exhaustive, particularly when their findings establish patterns of interpretation. A given practice may be interpreted

and explained in a competent manner and still contain some
meaning which has not been dealt with. What has been defined, explained, and interpreted is only an expression of the
unique phenomenon which underlies whatever is explicable, definable, and interpretable. Moreover, are we really
right to speak of "interpretive science"? Can the work of Marx
and Freud be reduced to that?

So, how am I to survive?

Since I do not know precisely where I stand, how am I to
conduct myself? This was Descartes' question, and his solution
was a provisional morality. Clearly, ethics will not wait, nor
will the technical problems raised by man's immediate needs.
Theoretical problems may, however, be deferred. We can
delay both raising the questions and attempting to find solutions for them. Men lose thereby, but they often fail to realize
it.

Can metaphysical problems be postponed? Ivan Karamazov
would answer no, for if God does not exist, one is free to do as
one pleases. Since one has only a short existence, it is imperative to know whether one does indeed have full license. Then
again, one might conclude that it is impossible to find answers
or solutions to these problems. In this case, one is either carried
along by cultural values or one opposes them—each of which
comes to the same thing, namely, orienting oneself simply in
terms of what one finds in a given environment at a given
time. But in the name of what? One's own tastes, pleasures,
and particular values? Yet these are still the products of a
specific environment. No matter. Since the question is how

to live, different people will derive their values from different sources. The important thing is to find something to live by today.

The desire to live with a good conscience has its history and is perhaps the product of civilization. But holding on to what is important to me, even if it is the product of my environment, is the sole solution for living, until I finally encounter convincing values.

*If coherent criticism makes everything come
unglued, my only real security will come
from sticking to my deepest convictions—in
other words, from following my conscience.
My conscience may be somewhat uncertain,
but for lack of anything better, it is the most
trustworthy source of guidance I can find.*

If my concern with having a "good conscience" arises out of a cultural situation, then adhering to what is important to me —even if it is basically a cultural habit—seems to me the sign of healthy practice.

Everything really does come unglued. Nothing escapes the suspicions of a subtle and exacting questioner. Nowhere do I find a fulcrum which offers me real and definite security. My greatest security still resides in my remaining true to my conscience. But this conscience that I call my own is fashioned by the civilization to which I belong. To act according to my conscience means to act according to a reality which I may have constructed by interiorizing the needs of a given civilization.

Since I find no fixed point, any point that offers me a feeling of relative security will do because in the final analysis I am still aware that my conscience may be nothing more than the product of a culture.

My idea of the inner consistency of the criticism seems to transcend my conscience, which may merely be the product of civilization. In this way the criticism is not determined by cultural forms. One god emerges unscathed from this universal debacle, a god I was not on guard against: criticism of inner consistency and scope, which judges everything, which has an opinion on every matter, and which sets standards. But perhaps these standards are also cultural products? This consistency and the drive for conceptual unity may also be produced by our civilization. Should I be suspicious of my own conception of consistency? But suspicious of it in the name of what? In the name of a new requirement which closely resembles the very qualities I now question.

In the midst of requirements and aspirations all apparently open to question, the only point of departure open to me is also open to question and must be arbitrarily chosen for the comfort it affords me: to be true to my conscience.

So I find I am both a philosopher and a believer.

My religious practices have been successfully explained, yet within them there is an apparently irreducible believer whom the philosopher never stops questioning. The philosopher would like to clear up an essential point: is he to take the believer seriously in a definitive way or is he to be finished with faith once and for all? But life shows him that it is futile to hope for a clear answer to this difficult question.

Once the believer suspects that he may be prey to illusions, he too is a philosopher. Once the philosoper fails to completely explain a religious practice, he is a believer. Each of these men furnishes the other with his daily bread.

Thus, I find that I contain both of these men—I come to understand my own makeup. All I am doing is talking about what is happening. My problems are bound up more with my discourse on what is happening than with the events themselves. The thoroughness and precision I bring to bear are aimed at an explanation of first things. This discourse about my belief is an attempt to *articulate* a basic commitment. The apparent reduction of religious practices really only deals with fragments of the discourse about myself as a believer. If I follow any particular practice, then I am no longer discussing myself as a believer but how conditioned I am or how sick I am. It is a sick man or a neurotically-conditioned man discussing his religious practices. When I am sick, I talk in an unhealthy way about the healthy man I used to be or am going to be. But even the sickness is not all of myself at this time; it is something outside in conflict with myself, acting with the complicity of elements in me which are not myself.

Therefore, the question is "What is my discourse about?" Does it really speak about what it claims to speak? This necessarily leads to the next question: "How can I make sure it really speaks about what I mean it to?" Therefore, I concentrate on the further development of my discourse. The discipline it demands becomes the sole condition for reaching reality.

As I carry out this particular religious practice, I recognize that the discussion cannot advance without a confrontation between the believer and the philosopher. But progress is a dangerous concept. It seems to suggest an advance toward a fixed point, toward an absolute reality which the words should be able to express. We must emphasize that nothing is given, that everything is constructed, including the religious practice. The discussion tends either to buildup the practice or to destroy it. The believer has created the philosopher, and the philosopher has created the believer. The religious man's discourse creates God, and God creates him with his living discourse. If there is an absolute reality, it can only be the goal of our discussion, not its starting point. If I am a believer, it is God toward whom my words are moving. I attain freedom by recognizing myself as a cultural product and refusing to be satisfied. By discourse, the examination of my discourse, and the analysis of this examination lead to my ultimate freedom. And this is also the process whereby I find I am both a philosopher and a believer.

I would like to make another comment on the philosopher and the believer.[2] For many centuries the believer had the upper hand in the West, and the world felt the force of his attack. Then the situation changed. Subsequent to the triumphalism of the believer there followed confusion as he saw the world become less and less Christian. Today the world is attacking the believer, and the philosopher seems infected with triumphalism. Since the eighteenth century it is a new experience for the believer to have to take from the philosopher what the philosopher had to take from the believer for many centuries.

A philosopher, because I am always on
guard against myself as a believer.

I have already gone into this proposition in my discussion of
"I find that I am both a philosopher and a believer." Therefore, I will only stop here to define the idea of "being on
guard" against something. If I am on guard against something, I am afraid because I am aware of danger. Humanly,
fear arises at the appearance of a recognized danger. In this
case, I am afraid of being mystified or deluded by the believer in me. The believer is always a dangerous man: his
faith makes him risk turning weakness into power, converting
conviction into conquest, becoming intolerant in his encounters with others. It is useless to draw up a list of the
misdeeds perpetrated in the name of religious belief. But the
worst of them seems to me the mishandling of truth: self-
deception with regard to what one believes he has found
and misuse of what one has found (or thinks he has found).
The believer can be the best of men, but he can also be the
worst. In mistrusting the believer at his worst, I can approach
belief.

Therefore, we must study the conditions involved in an
answer to the question Jesus asked Simon Peter; in meeting
this question I approach belief. If I reply, "I believe you are
God (or the *Son of God,* or the *Son of Man*)," how did I
arrive at that? Such an answer to Jesus of Nazareth indicates
that his testimony agrees with my concept of God and calls
for my adherence. My answer presupposes that I already have
some idea of God. Therefore, two factors determine my answer: first, the testimony of Jesus; second, my particular con-

cept of God. But this concept I have of God is also the product of the civilization that formed me. I will recognize God only if the testimony I accept fits the mold my civilization has given me. Most Jews did not recognize Jesus of Nazareth because he did not correspond to their concept of God.

My eventual recognition of God takes place at the conjunction between a testimony and a very personal and probably quite implicit concept of God. Conceivably, one man's testimony might be an infallible sign of divinity to me, provided it corresponds exactly to my idea of God. My answer to the question of Jesus, then, is no guarantee of anything. And yet such an answer could usher me into belief.

These are the factors involved in belief, and they put the philosopher on guard. The believer's explanation of his conviction is bound to be an imperfect and clumsy affair. His adherence is based on a decision and, hence, in part is not subject to analysis by the philosopher. When the believer is forced to account for his decision, he can only stammer.

Kierkegaard said that "The 'community of believers' becomes at last a courtesy title."[3] This is an apt expression in the present context, for we have come to think that as believers we do not know what we are doing, or why we are doing it, or how we ought to do it.

This is why we say to the philosopher that God continually confronts us. We must make this understood and draw a clear distinction between what ought to be rejected in our statement about God and what must remain. But Kierkegaard's remark is also a criticism and a cry for more lucidity. If the believer cannot help but speak nonsense, it is nonetheless important for him to understand why he cannot be other than what he is and how his dialogue with the philosopher should go on despite this—even because of this.

*A believer, because the Christian message
concerns and challenges me personally.*

At what moment can I consider myself a "believer"? As soon as I take seriously Jesus' question to Simon Peter, without necessarily committing myself once and for all. *Belief, in short, would mean believing in the seriousness of a question.* This seems to be *a minimal but adequate definition* of belief. Concerning my progress as a believer, I feel I cannot say much more of importance.

From this point on, I read certain things in one way and others in another. For example, I do not read the Gospel as I read Plato. Plato interests me, inspires me, or bores me, but I feel free to put him down without a bad conscience. I do not feel free to discard the evangelical values in the same way. What the Gospel sets forth concerns me; it has the ring of something which has been personally asked of me. Plato proposes ideas to me, but Jesus calls me. To encounter the Gospel resembles exposure to Kant's categorical imperative. I am the one in question, under obligation, and concerned.

But what do we mean by *to be concerned?*

We mean that something is offered to me and I have *no option* regarding whether to accept it: I cannot turn away because I am involved; moreover, if I did, I would be cheating. If someone tries to persuade me of something which does not concern me, I can ignore him with a clear conscience. The fact that something does concern me indicates my *connivance* with the thing in question, a sort of co-relation; it affects my being because to some extent we share the same substance. This means a union of the exterior and the interior, of that which is offered me and of my own desire, of that which comes in to me and of that which my discourse goes out to construct. I could say that in a certain way it is only myself which concerns me. If I feel concerned about something, it is because it raises a question about myself, about my life and my future. This does not mean that the something which concerns me is pleasant, or that I approve of it. I find many things pleasant which do not concern me—although my concern for them may begin as they start to please me—and many things which disturb me do concern me. I cannot escape this relationship.

Therefore, something concerns me because this something and I are *related existentially*: I could not give a serious account of my existence without taking it into account. This is why I cannot respond to something which concerns me as I respond to other things. From this standpoint I can say that certain passages in Plato concern me, while certain passages of the Gospel apparently do not—which seems to contradict what I said earlier. But if I want to carry this assertion further, I might say that I cannot be satisfied with fragmentary "concerns." I must take my stand on the essence of a message, and the essence of the Christian message is the "good news of salvation" brought to all men by Jesus of Nazareth, the Son of Man, as witnessed by his acts and life values offered to men. All of this is told by the first Christian generations in the collection of books which later Christians call the New Testament.

The essence of the Platonic message is a vision of the world, an exposition, through the noble Socrates, of a method of conduct with respect to oneself, others, and everything in the discourse. I am interested in Plato's vision of things, his view of man and the world; often he impresses me deeply or inspires me, but the essence of his message does not concern me. The only thing that concerns me is the Socratic method. Here I find the reality which concerns me, impressing itself on my *concern*. To be concerned with Socrates would mean to be in a living and dedicated relationship with the questions he leads me to raise. To be concerned with Jesus would mean the same thing, but it so happens that among the questions he leads me to raise there is one in particular which has a special ring of concern about it: "What is your position as to who I am?" I am concerned with the question Jesus asked Simon Peter: this is my point of emergence as a believer; the question is seen at a little distance from me, and it is seen solely through my consciousness of it.

How would my life develop if I affirmed my belief in Jesus Christ as the true Son of Man? In rough terms, this is how I see it. With time I have grown familiar with the Christian life, absorbing it from my civilization, education, environment, and habits. What I have learned represents a certain number of reflexes, concepts, and standardized behavior patterns in defined situations of social and private life. I have been taught that there is an all-powerful God who is infinitely good; that his only Son, Jesus Christ, appeared among men two thousand years ago; that he proclaimed the "Good News of salvation" in Palestine; that he suffered and died for us; that the one, holy, Catholic, Apostolic, and Roman Church was founded by him; that the Church will be the living representation of his life among us until the Parousia; that through the sacraments the Church perpetuates the living presence of Christ in the lives of Christians; that the Church has a mission to make the Good News known in Christ's name through faithful and vigorous preaching; that the Church is authorized to determine whether this mission is being properly executed as well as to organize Christians under the responsibility of bishops to assure the realization of the mission and the fruition of Christ's life in the Christian people. Here is an outline of some essential aspects of the convictions which have been impressed upon me since my childhood. I draw up this list without claiming that it is exhaustive.

For many years I lived in the climate of these religious convictions without asking myself serious questions, or if I did, I was sure that those who brought me up knew the answers. I had faith in my instructors because I did not dream that they could mislead *me*. But this also meant that from my standpoint as a child I did not think it possible that they could mislead *themselves* in serious matters. Yes, I used to believe in Santa Claus, but when I discovered that it was all a hoax, I took it for what it was: a kindly hoax. Yet this did not hold for religious matters; I could not conceive of being taken in or that my elders could be mistaken. Besides, I took the testimony of very kind or good people for a sign of truth. My first crisis came with the testimony of evil people. When I saw that evil people could subscribe to the existence of God or affirm that Jesus Christ is God I had my first doubts, or at least I began asking deeper questions.

In short, the years passed, some with all sorts of crises, some without. For good or ill, I lived in contact with the Gospel, now close to it, now at a certain distance from it. Things went on this way until a relatively late date when suddenly the question Jesus asked Simon Peter was personally put to me: "Who do you say that I am?" Not that it was put to me in these very terms, but one day I found that this question *concerned* me. And so I gave my answer: "Yes, I believe that you are who you claim to be. Since I have been nourished by you for so long, preoccupied with what you demanded of me, I believe that it is truly possible, that it ought to be very seriously considered, that it is probable or certain that you are the Son of God or, leaving exegetic questions aside, the Son of Man."

I cannot fully justify this adherence, any more than I can fully justify the fact that I love someone. And yet I cannot call my adherence irrational; it grew during my long familiarity with the essence of Christ's demands. It is *because I am nourished by them,* or try to be, that I can say yes to him. It is not, however, an unconditional Yes, for *a long period must be spent in considering what such a Yes means,* that is, *in pondering who Christ is,* before I can take my definitive stand regarding who he is. Therefore, I cannot go so far as to say that my adherence is irrational.

If I did say that my adherence is irrational, I would not be doing justice to what I am living, to my experience. On the other hand, I would readily admit that my adherence is ineffable, just as the why and wherefore of love is ineffable: this is not tantamount to saying that love exists without a reason.

To become a believer means to have traveled this road, to have heard the question put to Simon Peter and to have answered it as a question which concerns oneself; it means that at the very minimum I believe I must give very serious thought to the possibility that Christ is really who he claims to be.

But this raises another question. Does my answer imply that I already believe in God?

No, for I could be an atheist and still be impelled by Christ to raise the question of God. Do I dare confess that *on the level of my existence* my own personal pathway to God goes through Christ? In becoming more familiar with Christian values I take Christ's proclaimed identity more and more seriously, as I do the beliefs about him held by the first generations of Christians.

In other words, I first make contact with God's essence; only then is he revealed to me as an existent. No doubt God is the only Personal Existent, the only Living Thing, to be sought and found in this way. I know God through the nature of the living Christ, but in the case of all other personal beings I know of their existence before I know their essence.[4]

Perhaps this operation, this manner of proceeding from knowledge of essence to knowledge of existence, will be mistaken for what is usually called the ontological argument. But I do not find any far-reaching similarities between it and the ontological argument of classical philosophy. If some similarity were to be found, it would relate to certain remarks which have been made about St. Anselm's *Proslogium* and remarks about the true meaning of his views, not the misinterpretations of him which have prevailed since the Middle Ages. We must emphasize that St. Anselm places inquiry concerning God's essence after, not before, adherence through faith. This is where his readers have gone astray. St. Anselm begins with this premise: *It is true* that God exists, that God is the supreme being, that he is the threefold personification of one being, that he appeared in the flesh, etc. Then, St. Anselm goes on to discuss the problem of knowing "how far it is true."[5] And no doubt misinterpretation of St. Anselm stems from one's not taking into account "what . . . [he] does not say."[6]

I feel I must point out these details so that I myself will not be misinterpreted. Karl Barth has written a penetrating book on the proof of the existence of God; he closes with these words:

That Anselm's Proof of the Existence of God has repeatedly been called the "Ontological" Proof of God, that commentators have refused to see that it is in a different book altogether from the well-known teachings of Descartes and Leibniz, that anyone would seriously think that it is even remotely affected by what Kant has put forward against these doctrines—all that is so much nonsense on which no more word ought to be wasted.[7]

The fact of being concerned shows me that the inner and the outer worlds are related. Furthermore, my "concern" does away with this simplifying distinction. When we organize, reflect, rationalize, and create a theory for something, we go beyond this distinction, and expose its artificial and provisional nature. Once I become concerned with the world, when its ruptures and antagonisms cease, when things once foreign to me now raise an echo within me, I begin to perceive the world's unity. Where I once mistakenly saw isolated beings in juxtaposition, a discontinuous world with heterogeneous inhabitants, I now discover connivance and complicity, appeals and responses.

Reading the world through the eyes of reason, I discover a profound unity and cease to live in it as a stranger even if I do not immediately succeed in deciphering its greater reason. My being *concerned* with something means that I suspect a kind of relatedness between myself and things other than myself.

We have pictured the believer in a position of concern regarding evidence which could have remained foreign to him. For example we took the Christian face to face with Jesus Christ. We defined the Christian as a man who feels that he is concerned with Christ and with the testimonies of human societies and concrete texts about Christ.

This concern leads the individual to suspicion, and once suspicion is stripped of human products, to the serious question which he is then able to consider. A certain kind of answer will make the individual a believer.

My religious life is formed by this two-sided tension. The believer in me defies the philosopher, and the philosopher never succeeds in silencing the believer.

The believer exists only to the degree that he questions. The believer does not exist only because he cannot exist complacently. A believer who existed complacently would no longer be a believer. Complacent possession of truth is incompatible with belief. The philosopher too is an uneasy person. If he were not, he would be a sage. The believer and the philosopher continually rise from their ashes. The believer constantly comes to life again only because he constantly dies under the philosopher's assault. The philosopher constantly comes to life again only because he revives under the believer's assault. Death brings about rebirth for each of them. The philosopher constantly lays the believer's faith bare, changes it to something else, and dislodges it from its former position. But the believer raises new questions for the philosopher; the philosopher can never be completely finished with him. The philosopher's attacks lead the believer to discover new extensions to his questions. But after considering the philosopher's criticism and admitting that it is sound, the believer nevertheless says to himself, "Yes, but still. . . ." And the philosopher must then renew his efforts to reduce the believer.

This double operation characterizes the religious endeavor: God is affirmed, then denied because of his intangibility, then this negation is denied in turn in order to reach a new position, also destined to be denied, and so on indefinitely—and so the process goes from a position that is at best precarious to a negation that does not want to yield. And yet for all this, the discourse is not futile, for it sooner or later clears away the the illusions surrounding all the things it examines. It demythologizes. This kind of alternating discourse seems vital to a non-suspect religious *experience,* for such an experience can never affirm itself on its own merits, just as negation can really only affect something which is not itself. This experience cannot be expressed without having to be denied, nor can it be denied without having to be expressed.

This is the dialectic I am striving to analyze,
because this dialectic is the essence of my
religious experience: How is such a dialogue
possible? What foundation does it have?

The philosopher keeps an eye on the believer's practices; he examines the conditions behind the believer's Yes. He destroys many of the believer's illusions. He does this, yet this is *not all* he does. He locates the mystery behind the believer's Yes. But this Yes is not an inescapable conclusion reached by a well-regulated process that shuttles along through causes, consequences, and proofs. The reasons I may give someone else for my Yes are not enough to bring this Yes about. Something else is at play. When the question concerns the possibility of God's existence, the mechanics of reason are not enough; another factor enters in. The philosopher attacks ostensibly religious practices and destroys everything in them that is not specifically religious; the believer is continually reborn from this devouring fire, denying what he yesterday considered serious.

This confrontation is a constituent pary of my religious endeavor. My practices can be religious only because they are not religious. I cannot even imagine such a thing as a fundamentally religious practice. If I could, I would have already met the living God face to face. As long as God stands veiled before me, I do not know what religious practices are. But the philosopher saves me because he is constantly pointing out what religious practices are not. Without the philosopher the believer would be secure in his illusions before his idols.

What conditions make such a dialogue possible? If one participant stated his criticism while the other replied by showing that the premises for this criticism were false or incomplete, we would be hearing a polemic, a dialogue between two philosophers, not one between a believer and a philosopher. If the believer, claiming that he is on a different level, were content to simply assert his faith to the philosopher in defiance of his criticism, there would no longer be a *dialogue* between them. The dialogue cannot be real unless it deals with those elements in the believer's practices that are subject to the philosopher's analysis and criticism. The philosopher's criticism reveals the believer's illusions. The fact that the believer's practices are not entirely religious is reason enough for a dialogue to take place. In the final analysis, one could say that a dialogue is not possible between the philosopher and the believer at the level of the believer's faith. But as long as the believer has not reached the goal of his endeavor, he is "obliged" to hold a dialogue with the philosopher. This is a fortunate obligation, for it causes him to seek a more authentic religious endeavor.

This dialogue is neither a polemic between philosophers for the purpose of sorting out the reduced from the non-reduced nor a fruitless exchange between a believer and a philosopher who are not talking about the same thing; it is a dialogue between the believer who is in the process of establishing his belief and the philosopher who puts his finger on everything that is not really religious in an ostensibly religious endeavor.

*First, this dialogue presupposes that both
men are worthy participants: the philosopher
accepts the believer as a worthy partner in
spite of everything, including Marx and
Freud; the believer accepts the philosopher
as a worthy partner, in spite of all the
condemnations over the centuries.*

What do we mean by worthy? What is a worthy participant? He is a serious and honest *seeker* in the meaning we have already given these terms. Let us take a closer look at the idea of a *seeker*: research pursued consciously and continually is one of the signs of seriousness and honesty; victorious possession is a bad sign. If we assume that dogmas may be true, we may say that instead of stifling research, they actually promote it. First, they deepen the meaning of a formulation, then develop and complete it, for history calls for a constant translation of formulas, for translations adapted to new ways of thinking. A complacent possessor of truth is not a worthy participant. The philosopher asks the believer to be honest, that is, thorough and precise with what he experiences, ever ready and wanting to reexamine his discourse in order to complete it. The believer asks the same of the philosopher, that is, asks him to recognize him, provisionally at least, as the original existent who, once he has relinquished those elements in his practices that rightfully succumb to the philosopher's assault, declares himself irreducible. What is left after this assault? Nothing, perhaps, but this is what should be examined and established. The believer ought to insist on this examination. For each of them, an intransigent past is the main obstacle to such a dialogue.

These thoughts bring us back to the need for an honesty directed by conscience. Of all the solutions we could adopt in the confusion of an ultimate examination, to follow an honest conscience is the least suspect.

"And this in turn presupposes that this
dialogue is a source of life, that it is the
necessary condition for religious progress;
that it essentially characterizes the religious
progress, that it is identical with my religious
life, because it enables me to approach God"

These words sum up what was said earlier. I will say something more about the word "characterize": this dialogue "characterizes" religious practices, which is to say that religious practices ought to be dialectical, for the philosopher's comments are essential to the believer's life. Without the philosopher there would be no believer; there would be merely an impulsive creature subject to countless unverified and obscure conditions. To proceed from one suspicion to another, leaving one only to discover the next, is the character of the religious endeavor. But is there a contradiction in the idea that a religious endeavor may be forever open to question and yet might enable one to approach God? On the one hand, I admit I am not entirely sure of the validity of my practices, and, on the other, I have no reservations about affirming that this endeavor will lead me toward God. This act of putting religious practices into question seems neither complete nor exhaustive; is it a *real* questioning? I doubt everything except the fertility of my doubts and the idea that these doubts prepare the way for an encounter. If I affirm God, doing so on the basis of an encounter documented in history, my recognition of a God known to history escapes the philosopher's criticism; he may put into question everything I do, but he cannot question this adherence, this action, whereby I take my stand as to the divinity of a historical person. Analysis of the religious endeavor removes the believer's act of recognizing God from the field of the philosopher's criticism.

III
R^2

FIRST I ought to define what I mean by "R²," and to do so I will briefly call to mind the steps of my project. I began with the Prose Poem in which I tried to express ideas which seemed to me important and essential; the words I used there were those which came most readily to hand. I then analyzed this text sentence by sentence, with an eye to the difficulties it might present, the assumptions it entailed, and the questions and convictions it brought out. This commentary has come to a close. Of course, I could have given it much more scope, but I expressly wanted this book to be a short one. I would like to stimulate some thinking. Thus, I propose a certain approach which is in itself an entire system and involves a method all its own. But I do not claim to have the answers or to establish a complete systematics.

R^2 is a new step in this effort: it is reflection squared, that is, a reflection on our initial reflection, the commentary. I will try to be more objective with respect to my enterprise; in so doing I hope to determine its meaning and to pick up anything which might have escaped notice. Those problems I have already dealt with I will try to locate in a context of more general problems. This will be necessary for a clearer picture of where one will be led by the conduct I suggest. I cannot be sure that I will be able to sort out all the implications of my commentary, but I undertake this analysis in the conviction that further exploration is needed.

Is R^2 meant to reveal something new or is it simply an extension of the commentary? Is it *another* reflection or an addition to the first? As it unfolds, it will be both of these, for in referring back to the commentary we will often find ourselves entering new avenues of thought. As we refer back, we may get the impression that we are anchored in the commentary; then too, our efforts to go beyond it, if they are unsuccessful, will strengthen this impression. This project is not easy. It requires great clear-sightedness and an alert mind which I cannot presume to have.

To begin, I will explain my approach to this section of the work. I will be dealing with images, themes, categories, and questions. Why? I have thought about the commentary and managed to come up with these four irreducible, constituent elements of my thought: irreducible because in the last analysis an image does not amount to a theme, even if images do float about among themes, nor is a theme an image even if expressed through images; irreducible because an image is not a category, and if our categories often rest on images, it is only when these categories transcend images that they can truly be called categories. As for questions, they are at the very source of the spiritual life. Neither image nor theme nor category constitutes a question. To question is the final recourse of the spiritual life; to create images, to reflect along lines suggested by certain themes, to think within certain categories, these are only secondary steps with respect to our initial questioning. But perhaps we will discover that the questions we ask proceed from a world of images, themes, and categories, in short, that they are the result of the particular way we organize experience at a particular point in history—an experience that is *language*. I have organized this section by trial and error. After failing at my attempt to reduce images to themes, themes to images, and so on, I resolved to isolate images, themes, categories, and questions. They seemed to form the matrix of my thought on this subject, and these reasons seemed sufficient to me for establishing these divisions, no longer subjecting them to further questioning, but gradually defining the way in which images, themes, categories, and questions are themselves the products of a world or of several worlds.

I. THE COST OF IMAGES

THE believer is subject to uncertainty. But his certainty is more suspect than his uncertainty, for his certainty merely relates to himself. His relationship to something Other than himself can only mean uncertainty, otherwise this Other would not be truly Other, but his own self-image.[8]

This is what John A. T. Robinson had in mind when he wrote, "The first thing we must be ready to let go is our image of God himself."[9] The obstruction between God and man is the image of God that man fabricates, and this is the reason why many "serious" believers feel a sympathy with atheists.[10] A person cannot become "serious" in his religious practices until he is freed from his images and ideas while he continues to be the witness to a living, personal, and unchallengeable relationship.

To desire without desire, to wait without expectations, can only mean that *hoping is not the same thing as imagining.* Hope becomes an illusion when we burden it with our images, and we reduce the value of our images when we assign them the sorry role of consoling us. My goal has been to strip my anticipation of God of all those subtle, hidden predispositions with which I was building up a happiness of my own making.

74

If a true anticipation of God exists, then it is an anticipation of NOTHING; whatever I may anticipate, I am only anticipating myself, and this is not anticipation of the Other. The philosopher demands that the believer strip away his images; if the believer anticipates, he must not do so with images of his own invention. This is what the philosopher is always quick to warn him about. The philosopher requires him to die in abandoning all his personal images; under this condition alone will faith truly become a testimony to the presence of an Other.

Images cost us nothing, and for this reason they cost us the seriousness of our discourse. It is easy to come up with images, and it is also easy to invent reasons for them. Does not the strength of our discourses rest on the strength of the images supporting them? Are we not the prisoners of our images more than the prisoners of our discourses?

What we are recommending here is iconoclastic, is it not? If a religious endeavor is to be serious, it must be freed of its images and its ideas insofar as they are products of man. A believer must let go of these products of his own making so that his religious endeavor can eventually be considered serious. We cannot express the completely Other with our images or our ideas, and we cannot make use of them again until we have reached a complete understanding of their role: they are irreplaceable and at the same time so inadequate as to be laughable.

If all that the believer sees is himself, the philosopher will take him to task for it and reduce his faith. But if the believer sees the *Other* rather than himself, the philosopher cannot take a firm stand against him. The philosopher can say to the believer, "What you see and describe is not Other than yourself; if there is someone Other than yourself, he cannot be encountered in the way you imagine. Perhaps you could encounter him under such and such conditions."[11]

Yet images are an essential attraction of life. The image is a powerful aid to speculation. It is important to the growth of the theoretical side of science and is very helpful, even if its ill effects are great. Civilizations are built with images, and mythology has served as the matrix for all human development. The image is the source of countless errors, yet without it nothing could have evolved. All of this goes without saying. I merely want to point out that we should not understand the necessity to transcend images as a prejudiced refusal to work through them. It is true that a time is coming when development will cease if we do not abandon these images. A time is coming when reason will be sufficiently established so that we can dispense with them,[12] when we can go beyond them, and when a reversion to them will necessarily cost us a certain decrease in their value.

The image plays a vital role in human life, but we should not make use of it again until we see it for what it is: a world which commands a select place among man's creations, games, and arts; of these, the image is the most capable of filling us with enthusiasm, (in the etymological meaning of this term, hence, the most capable of filling us with "divine fervor"). Through the magic of images alone does a person become himself. Without them he would die. Through images a world is created where life is possible, a world constructed just as we would have it. It is not a question of foregoing images, but of appreciating them for what they are: humanity's most prestigious product.

This is why we waver fascination with the images we fall
prey to and an iconoclastic revolt against them all. But is it not
wrong to feel we must make a choice?[13] Why should we have
to? If our idea needs an image for its expression, if our image
contains an abundance of ideas, why not respect both and
define their exact function? If images proceed from our weak
reasoning power or if our images are richer than our ideas, then
we have reached an impasse. We have a chance to solve this
dilemma by looking at the problem as a dynamic affair: if our
images are rich, they will project us into the world of ideas; if
our ideas are rich, they will project us into the world of images,
the only domain where they can attain expression. It would
mean death to be riveted to images or ideas *which one could
not get beyond;* the images would then oppose the ideas, and
the ideas the images. If we take an image or an idea for what
it is, we cannot stay with it for long. I mean to reject here the
image-prisons which confine man to a dead world in which
nothing new can arise. Yet at the same time I can only praise
those images which are filled with enthusiasm—enthusiasm in
its root sense, fervor inspired by a divine being—and which
lead us on to an infinite number of discoveries, to a life in full
expansion where every reality we discover implies another to
be found beyond it. The images we must let fall are thus recovered, for "man is incapable of experiencing anything what
soever *without expressing it,*" and "once we have understood
that God cannot appear or speak or present himself to our
sensibilities, there is nothing to stop us from making him
appear, speak, and become involved in the world of sensibility.
This is the only way we can translate into words that which
transcends all discourse."[14] The one thing I am asking here
is that these images be demythologized, that is, taken for what

they are—products of man—and that they be authenticated, that is, that words, ideas, and images concerning God proceed from their one serious origin—God. The only valid foundation for man's discourse on God, if God steps forth, is God himself speaking the language of man.

The preceding thoughts tended to illustrate the necessity for discarding our images and then went on to suggest that this necessity does not mean that images are completely worthless. I wanted to show that once one has gained some distance from them, there is no reason why he cannot make some use of them again; this can be done as long as there is no further danger of his being mystified by them. Under these conditions, not only can we go back to these images, and this is a kind of concession, but they can become an essential dimension of our power to create. This is more than a concession to use them; it is an invitation to use them.

However, there is a remark in the commentary which we must define: *Expectations without images belong on the level of accomplishment and fulfillment.* Exactly what does this mean? I mean a return to desire, but a desire which does not invent its object. I had to stress the necessity of ridding oneself of images; however, one does not have to quell his desire in order to keep it from inventing its object, for desire continues even after the destruction of the illusory images it produced. There is still a desire which we can experience in its pure state, without the aid of images and without knowledge of its object; it is a kind of dynamic existence gravitating toward some kind of accomplishment, a striving toward an anticipated fullness which one cannot picture. This is what I meant by the idea that anticipation without images is accomplishment, is fullness.

Thus, the images we have let fall are recovered as invitations to human creation. We now encounter them on another level and with a different function. Yet precision and thoroughness depend on our avoiding them as objects invented by our desires. It is a question of an image turning into a thing, not of desire losing itself in an image incapable of becoming a reality.

2. THEMES

THEMES CONCERNING THE HORIZONS OF OUR PRACTICES

A problem without a solution

What makes a religious endeavor possible? This is the question we have been dealing with from the beginning of this study. If we decide that the answer cannot be given as simply, say, as a cooking recipe or a doctor's prescription, our approach must take a special turn. An important theme of this book has been *the usefulness and effectiveness of a question which does not have a clear-cut answer,* a problem which merely leads to deeper insight into its premises or to a fresh formulation of them, although this insight and formulation are unable to conduct us to a satisfying solution. We will give this theme special attention.

To find a solution would mean to give an account of the believer's adherence at the level of philosophic criticism. But if the explanatory discourse of the philosopher were able to contain this adherence, such adherence would no longer be what it was intended to be: now it would merely be the conclusion of a purely mechanical process involving a certain number of given conditions. Does the forming of a judgment merely consist in an act of understanding, or is something more implied? Can wishing be reduced to understanding, or are other forces at play?

We find that intensification of dialogue is profitable to the philosopher and the believer alike, even if it does not lead to an enumeration of the exact conditions of the believer's adherence and even if such conditions must always be studied anew. Although it will not lead to conclusions, we will have gained for being more exacting in our efforts; we will have demythologized false modes of adherence or deceptive divinities.

The fulfillment of faith would mean its death. The believer is incomplete as long as he pursues the question. There is still no answer to the problem of his role and status with respect to the philosopher. The latter perseveres in his effort to reduce the believer, constantly renewing his efforts to define the conditions for a serious faith. Yet the philosopher is no more able to reach a conclusion than is the believer, for adherence cannot be stabilized. Stabilization could only occur through a direct vision of God, and this in itself would spell the death of faith. Therefore, religious practices raise a problem without a clear-cut solution, for the solution would entail a negation of the premises of the problem.

Perhaps man's life and youth are better suited to doubt than to systems or to an establishing the self in the truth. Let us consider Kierkegaard's young doubter:

I do not mean that every youth can vanquish Hegel, far from it; if the youth is conceited and foolish enough to attempt it, his attack will be without significance. No, the youth must not even think of attacking Hegel. On the contrary, let him submit himself unconditionally, in feminine devotion, but with sufficient vigor of determination to hold fast to his problem: he will become a satirist without suspecting it. The youth is an existing doubter. Hovering in doubt and without a foothold for his life, he reaches out for the truth—in order to exist in it. . . . But a philosophy of pure thought is for an existing individual a chimera, if the truth that is sought is something to exist in. To exist under the guidance of pure thought is like travelling in Denmark with the help of a small map of Europe, on which Denmark shows no larger than a steel penpoint . . .[15]

For existing beings, to strive to exist in the truth is to trade one doubt for another. Pure, abstracted, and established truth is only a chimera. For man, the condition for truth is an experience, one which must be lived as a never-ending question, as practices which are never complete. The human condition for truth is one in which reaching a conclusion would merely mean embracing an abstraction.

The change of problematics

What is meant by the problematics of a question? Problematics denotes the cluster of historical circumstances prompting human groups to raise a given question in a given manner. There is a correspondence between questions and factors in the historical environment—between questions and a certain way of viewing the world, of interpreting one's findings, of reacting, etc. This complex differs from age to age, and it explains how a question will arise in a given epoch or milieu, arise and be met by an answer or by several answers.

We will examine what appears to be a breakdown in communication between the philosopher and the believer, a breakdown due to a difference in problematics. Although the
philosopher and the believer operated in the same social
background, they have been separated from each other by
changes in the world.

"Classical" problematics focused the debate on the relationship between the concept of faith and the concept of reason.
It was thought that there were two worlds, one dominated by
faith, the other by reason. The question of their respective
domains could have led to centuries of analysis, elaborations
of systems and subsystems, quarrels alternating between in-
transigence and tolerance, between outright rejection and
concession.

For example, the question, "Can one demonstrate the existence of God through reason?" made sense in classical problematics, but does it have meaning today, now that the
problematics has changed? We are living in a period which
follows Marx, Freud, and Einstein. We stand on the devas-
tated landscape of our extinguished dreams, asking ourselves
about the seriousness of the question of God. In the world we
are living in, faith is occasionally known as something other
than obstinacy, as something other than an attachment to
traditions designed to ward off the perils of a new world, as
something other than a refuge or a watchful fear of terrible
forces and the torment of eternal suffering. And what is this
new faith all about, now that its timeworn aims have van-
ished? Man finds himself the creator where he once thought
of himself as the created, and from this time forward this
creation stands before us as an appeal to action, an appeal
which must be answered right away.

A problematics is not chosen. We are men of our times, and the questions we put to ourselves belong to the times we live in. Can we blame modern men for feeling no identification with questions which were being raised at the close of the nineteenth century or at the beginning of the twentieth? Many people today cannot help smiling when they hear the question, "Can one demonstrate the existence of God?" On the other hand, the question would be authentic if one asked, "Can the question of God be a serious question, and if it is a serious one, what are the conditions which allow it to be so?"

To refuse a change of problematics is to betray today's humanity in the name of attitudes belonging to yesterday's humanity.

What exactly were the "classical" proofs for the existence of God? In this chapter we are summoned to the concept of a *problematics*. Every question presupposes a problematics, including the classical proofs for the existence of God, themselves inseparable from their particular problematics. By classical proofs I mean the five Thomist proofs: proof by movement, proof by causality, proof by the existence of contingent beings, proof by the degrees of perfection of beings, and proof by the order in the world. The problematics of these classical proofs presupposes a homogeneous world, that is, a world whose principles of phenomenal reality can be applied to metaphysical realities. It implies an absolute world, that is, a world of three dimensions in which realities are what they seem to be, untouched by questioning, beyond all relativity. A problematics leads to an analysis of the historical conditions of a question. The arguments for the classical proofs of the existence of God arise from the question, "Is it possible to demonstrate the existence of God through reason alone and without the aid of grace?" This question presupposes a theological problematics which was quickened by sharp debates—especially in the nineteenth century—and by fluctuations of theological thought between fideist and rationalist positions on the subject of theodicy. This was the question the First Vatican Council answered in its assertion that

The one holy Church, our mother, holds and teaches that God, the principle and end of all things, can be known with certainty through the application of the natural light of human reason to created things: *ever since the creation of the world his invisible nature has been clearly perceived in the things that have been made* (Rom. 1:20).[17]

And we find in the Anti-Modernist oath of 1910 the same thought: "I profess that God, principle and end of all things, can be known with certainty, and therefore can be demonstrated, *in the things that have been made* (Rom. 1:20) through the natural light of reason, that is, in the visible works of creation, as the cause can be known through its effects."[18]

Thus, the question was purely theological: "Is it possible to demonstrate the existence of God through reason alone and without divine grace?" Now then, our question is not the same: "Under what conditions can the question of God be raised in a serious way?" This new question reflects the fact of our living in a historical context which has become consciously post-Marxian and post-Freudian; it assumes that we have accepted the validity of a series of criticisms and analyses of certain aspects of our religious practices and that our problem is one of discovering how we can conduct a religious en-

deavor which is valid *in the philosopher's eyes*. Our problem
is not whether one can succeed, without divine grace, in
demonstrating the existence of God *to other believers and the
Church*. The debating parties have changed, the historical
conditions have changed, and the question itself is different.
Put in crude terms, my point is this: the question asked of the
Fathers of the First Vatican Council in 1870 had its own particular problematics. Does this question still have meaning
when put to philosophers today, men who may be atheists and
who are subject to a problematics which has nothing to do
with that of the Fathers of the First Vatican Council? We
must reply that this question has no meaning to those for
whom it is intended. Therefore, if we aspire to thoroughness
and precision, we must hold to the idea that every question has
its problematics and must be considered within it and *cannot
be transposed into another one*. Any given question has a corresponding problematics which we should track down; if the
problematics has changed, the question has lost its meaning.
Then, the question the philosopher asks today should be not
whether one can demonstrate without divine grace the existence of God. Rather, the question should be, "What are the
conditions which will make for serious religious practices
free from all mystification?"

The irruption of God

When man takes the initiative, his discourse on God becomes
a discourse on himself; therefore, a meeting with God cannot
be serious unless it is God who takes the initiative. If an
Other is there, standing in front of man, it is up to this Other

to reveal himself, to speak and make himself understood. God is an irruption, an unanticipated occurence in man's life. All anticipations are in reality only anticipations of oneself.

I want to live, but I do not need God in order to live. The world is large, broad, and beautiful, and it offers me everything I need for my temporal fulfillment. It suits me, I love it as it is, and I feel that it is made for me as I am made for it. When I say the world, I am speaking of the world as a whole, with everything it contains and with all the beings that people it. A world to build, a world with friendship, love, discovery, creative work—I could not ask for more. When I look at it from this point of view, I do not need God; my desire to live has nothing to do with a desire for him. But does the world have a hidden desire for God? Nowhere is it evident. Dissertations on desire for God read like an apologetic artifice that does injustice to this perfect exchange between man and the world, between man and man. The world has the means to make man happy, and his relationship to his fellows can be a true end in itself. God is a superfluous luxury, an afterthought, a personage we address more out of curiosity than out of spontaneous need.

What do we mean when we speak of a desire for God? If man's basic desire is for life, as I have just suggested, then it is up to God to show himself if he wishes to be known, loved, and desired by man. And since the world is so well-suited to man, and man is nicely suited to it and to his fellows, what place does a desire for God have in man's life? The creative perspectives are such that man has no need for anyone but man; if God wants man to need him, it is God's responsibility to act, since the world is so constructed that God can be absent from man's life without man's actually suffering. Therefore, if God wants to be desired by man, it is up to him to act— God the creator and all-powerful, the personal God whose desire no one could refuse to carry out, to whom no one can assign limits.

Everything in the history of the Christian revelation seems to indicate that God wants to be discovered and gratuitously loved. God alone has the prerogative of making himself known, but once he has done so, and a man comes to love him, an astonishing thing happens: the man begins to need this God who has made himself known, although he never really needed him before. This man finds someone unexpected on his path, someone who speaks his own language and offers him friendship; this man is astonished, and begins to desire the God whom he did not know or need, looking to him with deep love. And this God, who is loved for himself, who is loved gratuitously, then steps forward to bounteously satisfy this man's true desire—the desire for eternity. This is what a man misses in his possession of the world, what he misses in his relationship with others. He misses an unexpected personage who reveals himself, makes himself known, loved, desired, doing this out of friendship and as a gratuitous act.[19]

But is such optimism permissible? If we avoid inventing a God who supplies us with the missing element in our lives, are we not in danger of closing our eyes to all the tangles in the world, to all the snarls in history? Could it not be said that confusion and even chaos belong to our experience of this world as much as do fullness and harmony? "Nature is not in itself geometrical, and it appears so only to a careful observer who contents himself with macrocosmic data. Human society is not a community of reasonable minds, and only in fortunate countries where a biological and economic balance has locally and temporarily been struck has such a conception of it been possible."[20] But the taste for reality is less suspect than a possible distaste for it, and certain situations are less subject to illusion than others. This is why the time of fullness is more likely to allay our suspicions about God's possible irruption.

In any case, we have felt it important to show that God cannot step forth through human efforts. We do not prepare for the advent of God; God appears like a flash. And images only prevent us from recognizing him. God alone is capable of giving us true images and ideas of himself. This is the framework in which a Holy Scripture can attain philosophical status. There definitely is philosophic justification for the idea that a Holy Scripture or an Incarnation can be the sole foundation for human discourse on and human images of God. If God is not a product of man, he will appear as the Unanticipated. And any discourse on God, if serious, will presuppose the dawn of revelation.

There is a remark in the commentary which might be challenged: "The Other is not anticipated. In childhood one is caught up with the self, anticipates the self only. But becoming an adult means encountering the Other—this presence we cannot anticipate—and loving him." How can we affirm the Other as an unanticipated being? If he is unanticipated, we cannot speak of him. The unanticipated can only be affirmed after he has been encountered. We find echoes here of St. Anselm: only the believer who in faith has already met God can assert, through analysis of his attributes, that he exists. We call the Other unanticipated because the believer has already met him and speaks only of *an experience he has had*. How can we say anything at all about an unanticipated reality, let alone maintain we love it? The question comes down to asking whether we can love something we do not know. Now it is a natural characteristic of human love to be directed toward an Other, a free presence who always escapes us. And the Other, being free, can never be contained by our knowledge. To love someone always means to love the unanticipated. And the unanticipated, if a person, even after having been met, continues to be the unanticipated.

God can speak, but it is not up to us to make him speak. All the philosopher can do is to demythologize the human discourses which are presented as discourses on God. At this point in our reflection we should repeat that the believer has a theory of the Gospel which is of utmost interest to the philosopher. If it is true that God has spoken, how did he do so? And how can we explain this incredible relationship between God and a sacred writer who expressed God's very words? This is one of the essential points on which the philosopher is going to judge the believer.

Still, how can I speak of an irruption of God? Either my affirmation that God is there is suggested to me by material in my culture, in which case there is no true irruption, or my affirmation already contains *something more* than what my cultural environment has led me to adopt. But what can be the basis for this idea if it is not experience? The question that is really being asked here is whether I have in fact experienced God: either the invasion is based on this original, irreducible experience or it is an illusion, a pseudo-irruption which I take for a real one in order to support my enterprise.

This concept of an irruption was to help me in my determination to be thorough and precise in locating the question of God, but now I find that it may contain some doubtful elements. If the concept is to be of some use, it must be the echo of a pure and irreducible experience, not an invention to support material given me by cultural environment.

The meaninglessness of the question of God's existence when raised by man

The question of God is troubling to the philosopher. His difficulties with it stem from the fact that the very raising of the question already implies an idea of God, an idea which is itself a human product. The question, "Does God exist?" goes hand in hand with another: "Can I assert the existence of a being whose image I myself have created?" Thus, the concept of God is something like a hypothesis which I must accept or reject, but a hypothesis presented to me by the civilization I grew up in. I take my stand on a certain idea of God which a human environment gives me. Therefore, I will have to decide about the hypothesis of God in the same way I will about any hypothesis stemming from intellectual speculation. I have no reason to reject this procedure, but it nevertheless cannot be conclusive or lead me to an affirmation free from doubt. Once again I reach the idea that the meeting with God cannot be decisive unless God's initiative comes as an irruption into my life. And this in itself is saying too much. If I speak of God's initiative, I already conceive of God as a personal and self-willed being, and this is going too far.

Am I almost sure that God exists? I think so . . . and yet it is difficult to make the question of God a serious question. Let us sum up what we have said. To ask the question, "Does God exist?" is already cheating; I already have a certain idea of God. What I am really asking is, "Does my idea of a certain God correspond to something real?" or, "Does the God I conceive of exist?"

If the question is to be serious, I will not have to ask it. God cannot be an existent whose existence I question. The question of God as formulated by me is illusory and can only have meaning when formulated by someone else. But by whom? Either by God as an irruption in my life, as he reveals himself to me, or by a cultural environment conveying to me a certain notion of God—a notion which I question. It must be said that this second way of formulating the question is not very genuine, for if the question is to be accepted as valid, we must admit that my culture will have communicated its notion of God to me, mystifying me because the notion merely mirrors the culture. Would this not change the question to, "How does man conceive of God?"

If the question of God is not to be suspect, it must undergo a most difficult purification and a harsh stripping away; if it is to be correctly formulated, it cannot be formulated by man. We must now consider whether God himself does not put this question to man. The question of God is the most difficult one a person can be asked in that it may be the most mystifying.

In considering how God might put this question to man, we are in danger of slipping into an artificial dialectical game: does this formulation take place through the "exterior" or the "interior"? Some will maintain that God puts the question to man through exterior means—revelation. Others will argue that he makes use of interior means; they will say that man is much more than man, that God can be perceived by, and even dwells in, the deepest elements of the human being. But in a post-Marxian, post-Freudian, and post-Einsteinian context, it seems difficult to go back to these spatializing concepts; their aim is to localize God, and they lead to false problems. The surest concept visualizes a *presence.* Then, the question is to know what the presence of God means and how man can be a witness to it. This takes us back to the concept of experience. A dialectics involving the "exterior" and the "interior" or the "outer" and the "inner" leads us into too many problems, problems arising from images which spell danger to us rather than profit.

We are obliged to consider the possibility of an experiencing of this Other presence; it would be the sole justification of the question of God. The problem here would be to make a discourse on this presence valid for other people. As a rule, the mystical experience alone justifies our question of God. But how is it to be validated? If this presence is valuable to oneself alone, one cannot address his discourse on God to others.

Is it possible to have a meeting or some communication about individual mystical experience? Such communication would not involve images or even the mystical experience itself; it would be communication in affirmation of a presence, and would be achieved through a complete stripping away of images and a negation of all discourse. Although we are at a total loss for words to describe this Other presence, communication would be established in our extreme awareness of it in the very fabric of our prosaic everyday life.

In short, the question of God is serious only if it is formulated by someone other than myself. Either the concept of God is a product of myself and of the human environment of my life, and I question its seriousness, or this question is put to me by God himself, and we have found the *one and only* condition for the seriousness of the question. All else is chimera. The problem is to learn whether this question is mine or the Other's; this, and this alone, determines whether the question can be reduced.

Moreover, if the question of God is put to me by God, and if I am to understand it, it must be expressed in *my* language. But my language is myself, which means that the question raised by God comes to expression through me. Thus, we find ourselves in a paradoxical situation: a question must be expressed by someone Other than myself, but if I am to understand it, it must become myself. The question must borrow the words of *my* discourse while assuring me that it owes nothing to the words of my discourse. This is why the theory that God addresses his word to man is one of the most important and difficult aspects of our understanding of the theandric relationship—important because it affects the seriousness of the question asked of man, difficult because all we can talk about is the condition which allows God's dialogue to be at once understandable to man and unrestricted by the words of the discourse.

Two things are equally true for the believer who has reached this point: "I cannot seek you if you do not show me how, or find you unless you show yourself to me."[21] Karl Barth expressed this in an admirable way in his analysis of St. Anselm's *Proslogium:*

A careful reading of the relevant text of the opening prayer of the *Proslogion* shows that all the way through what Anselm has in mind as the object of his request is twofold. The first of course is— that God would instruct his heart, *ubi et quomodo te quaereat,* that God would enlighten his eyes, that he who by nature ever stoops to earth might be lifted up to look on him. Here we cannot fail to recognize this aspect of grace as the actualizaton of that power to know which was originally created in man. But the occurrence of *intellectus* and therefore the requested grace has still another objective aspect. Anselm places alongside this request a second—it seems to me impossible to take it as a mere rhetorical repetition of the first in view of the whole tenor of the context—that God would instruct his heart *ubi et quomodo te inveniat,* that God would let him see his face, let him see his very Self. That God would give himself to him again. He interprets the plight of man in his failure to know God, a plight which even the believer shares, as being due to the fact that he is involved in the remoteness from God of a humanity that is sinful by inheritance. This remoteness is clearly an objective remoteness of God himself—God is absent, he dwells in light unapproachable. What is the man who yearns for him to do? *Anhelat videre te et nimis abest illi facies tua; accedere ad te desiderat et inaccessibilis est habitatio tua . . . Usequequo Domine oblivisceris nos, usquequo avertis faciem tuam a nobis? Quando respicies et exaudies nos . . . et ostendes nobis faciem tuam?* [He aspires to see you, and your face is far from his; he desires access to you, and your dwelling place is inaccessible. . . . How long, Lord, will you ignore us, how long will you keep your face averted from us? When will you look at us and hear us . . . when will you show us your face?][22]

There is, in fact, a contradiction in the idea of a human discourse on God, for it is impossible to have a human discourse

—one taking place in my language—which leaves man out of the picture. What is needed is a nonhuman-human discourse. Now then, since it will be addressed to me in my language, it will not be nonhuman because a discourse in my language must register in and through me, my language being myself. In the light of this insurmountable contradiction, we are forced to admit that man cannot express God.

THEMES CONCERNING PRACTICES

A journey without an absolute
point of departure

This inquiry is not a search for an absolute point of departure, for an unchallengeable, definitive certainty that could serve as the foundation for a solid edifice. We begin wherever we can, but wherever this beginning may be, the problem is always the same: all points of departure are *historical,* hence, necessarily relative. There was a time when we pined for an absolute point of departure, for all our efforts went into finding it.

But a relative point of departure is no longer considered such a bad thing. I myself accept it; in fact, I find it enormously helpful. If all endeavors depart from a historical context, then the exercise of thoroughness and precision on our journey is a better guarantee of consistency and seriousness than is an absolute point of departure, for all its stainless purity. Knowing so little about our origins, how will we set out and where will we find the source of our question? These are the real questions concerning the seriousness of our discourse.

The confrontation as a constituent of the
religious endeavor, and atheism as
philosophy's role

An idea has been flowing through these reflections in a fairly
surreptitious manner; it argues that the fact of seeking guarantees the quality of the endeavor. Neither the philosopher
nor the believer can bring his work to an end. Each constantly
raises new questions; the philosopher is never done with the
believer, nor the believer with the philosopher. The philosopher is challenged by the believer's question, and the believer
by the philosopher's, the latter's even being a challenge with
respect to God. For each of them, a solution would certainly
mean error; this is the very nature of the relationship between the finite and the infinite, between man and God,
between time and eternity. Both the philosopher and the believer are conscious of this, and have a horror of reaching
conclusions, for each knows that if he does, he will be untrue
to himself and fail. The death of the philosopher would spell
the death of the believer, and the reverse is probably true, too.

Thus, philosophy started to feel out its role. Leaving a God
it had taken little trouble to get to know, it began to look at
him with an inquiring eye, bringing high standards to its inquiry—thoroughness, precision—standards carried over from
experimentation in concrete subjects such as chemistry and
physics. From this point it gravitated toward the idea that
God is unknowable since it could not apply principles to him
whose claim to validity rests on the level of demonstration and
proof. But to pronounce God unknowable really makes him all
the easier to bypass: if he is unknowable, why not do without

him? And little by little, philosophy gave up a concept it considered useless. However, we could still ask, "Having reached this point, does philosophy call for the believer to disappear?"

The idea which emerges here is that philosophy, conscious now of its role as an atheistic force and developing it, does not call for any such thing; in fact, it actually establishes rigorous conditions for an authentic belief. In other words, we could say that if philosophy had not developed this atheistic principle, faith would have perished. By attacking all the images and ideas of God which were merely products of man, philosophy created indispensable conditions for an authentic hearing of a Word addressed to man. The believer thought he was losing himself at the very place where he actually found himself. But fear and inconsistency prevented the believer from taking up these rigorous requirements and putting them to good use, even though they were established currency in the domain of philosophy.

Philosophy claims the right to deal with the concept of God when this concept is a product of man. The believer has nothing to say in the matter. What is left to him? The possibility that one day he may stand up and say something about God, but about a God who is not produced by man. When that time comes, will the believer's endeavor fall outside the philosopher's jurisdiction? No, for the believer's endeavor, as a method, as an exercise of rigorous standards, still falls within the philosopher's jurisdiction. The philosopher will always have the right to criticize the believer's methods, to carry out examinations in the name of him whom the believer is talking about, to question the meaning of his discourse. Who is encountered? Only the believer can say. But the philosopher can exercise his right to examine all the details involved in this encounter; indeed, it may take him a lifetime to work out all the implications. The believer, if he is ever to become a "serious" person, must confront the philosopher.

Emptiness

Whatever is derived simply from human resources is a source of illusion for the believer. And the philosopher takes it upon himself to demythologize these false gods, and the creations of believers are put to flight. Our images and ideas may be the most difficult thing we grapple with in the course of our religious journey. If the believer is to be the witness to a presence which is not himself, he has no alternative but to strip himself of his images and ideas and to free himself completely from his own creations. Religious practices cannot be carried out with thoroughness and precision unless one begins with emptiness. Mystics are familiar with this idea, and the philosopher rediscovers what it means.[23]

Let us not attribute to God the universe of our ideas, the constellation of our values, still less our interests and opinions. God is not the sum of our representative pictures of the world, a light-beam made up of the thought-systems we project. His presence within us compels us to forge ideas and values, causes us to think and act, but we should not try to encompass it or possess it as one would a thing. "Analogies," however refined, are always too human in character; only the mystical night can give rise to true faith.[24]

We should not free ourselves from our images and our ideas only to replace them surreptitiously with *feelings*; certain authors seem to open themselves to criticism on this point. Here is an example of what I mean:

Grace . . . strikes us when we walk through the dark valley of a meaningless and empty life. It strikes us when we feel that our separation is deeper than usual, because we have violated another life, a life which we loved, or from which we were estranged. It strikes us when our disgust for our own being, our indifference, our weakness, our hostility, and our lack of direction and composure have become intolerable to us. It strikes us when, year after year, the longed-for perfection of life does not appear, when the old compulsions reign within us as they have for decades, when despair destroys all joy and courage. Sometimes at that moment a wave of light breaks into our darkness, and it is as though a voice were saying: "You are accepted. *You are accepted,* accepted by that which is greater than you, and the name of which you do not know. Do not ask for the name now; perhaps you will find it later. Do not try to do anything now; perhaps later you will do much. Do not seek for anything; do not perform anything; do not intend anything. *Simply accept the fact that you are accepted!*" If that happens to us, we experience grace. After such an experience we may not be better than before, and we may not believe more than before. But everything is transformed. In that moment, grace conquers sin, and reconciliation bridges the gulf of estrangement. And nothing is demanded of this experience, no religious or moral or intellectual presupposition, nothing but *acceptance.* In the light of grace we perceive the power of grace in our relation to others and to ourselves."[25]

This long quote should warn us that *there is a danger that we may reject our ideas and images only to replace them with a feeling.* And this feeling is as much a product of ourselves as

are the ideas and images we put behind us. Moreover, emptiness is never a state or a finished thing, but a goal for religious
practices to aim at; one constantly loses sight of it, one must
constantly reestablish one's bearing. Despit our best intentions,
intrusions are forever slipping in to thwart us in our effort to
reach this emptiness. We pursue our practices in a desert; if
images, ideas, or feelings are to feature in our activity, they
must stem from God. And this might well happen, for we are
thinking in terms of a word of the God-made-flesh, a Revelation, and a Holy Scripture. Moreover, the philosopher cannot
help but be extremely interested in anything the believer proposes in the way of a theory of the Scripture or of divine
inspiration; the philosopher considers such a work carefully in
order to determine whether elements in the believer's discourse are valid, for each man is well aware that this discourse
must be *a listening to God speak, not a making God speak.*
The seriousness of the believer's discourse is in question here,
and therefore his utterances on the subject fall in part under
the philosopher's jurisdiction.

This is the "stripped" state which St. John of the Cross
reaches on attaining "the destruction within himself of everything that is not God."[26]

A sudden solitude; here everything that is not God is dead. Looked
at from the point of view of man, the soul now resembles one of
those desolate mountains where John of the Cross asked the monk
to come to pray, one of those places *devoid of possibilities for
sensory recreation* and where the contemplative loses himself in
the terrain, he himself now resembling those grey, dead mountain
villages in Spain that blend into the structure of the rock and describe a sort of fusion of things and beings. But looked at from the

divine point of view, the soul in this state of nudity finds God himself. God insinuates himself into us when he finds us denuded of all that is not him. This leads to *the soul's being brushed in its substance by the loving substance of God.*[27]

This is the point when the word recovers its rights: we are living within the word, and cannot live a reality without expressing it in words, even when we know that our discourse does not do justice to what we are living. There is urgency to the word; it is ourselves. The presence which cannot be uttered is exacting. *We become the word through the knowledge that we ourselves have nothing to say.*

Good conscience derived from honesty and seriousness, or truth reached through practices

Classical *objectivity* has been replaced to a great extent by the application of high standards to the self and by what we call *authenticity* in the exercise of high standards. When people realized that objectivity *could not keep* its promise, they turned to authenticity, and, in their quest for thoroughness and precision, they tried to make it the keynote of their human endeavors. These two attitudes have a quality in common— *honesty,* which affords one a good conscience. For the classical scientific conscience, being objective means wanting to be honest, for being honest is essential to that conscience. For a scientific conscience which no longer believes in the myth of objectivity, the pursuit of high standards and authenticity is also the desire to be honest.

The history of scientific honesty is a history of our changing attitudes toward the attainment of a good conscience. Discovering the inanity of most of our discourses on God, John A. T. Robinson asks the believer to be exacting with himself in his religious endeavor; Robinson expects honesty, expressed in a striving for thoroughness and precision, to secure the integrity of the religious endeavor. *Honest to God* means that the refusal to cheat with our conscience is the means by which we can be sure we are being exacting with ourselves in our utterances about God. It means that as we face God, who always escapes us in that he is absolutely transcendent, honesty, however reducible our discourse, guarantees the validity of our religious practice.

Do we not find this same sort of attitude in Kant? Is there not an entire philosophy today whose final validity rests on one's having a good conscience as he carries out intellectual practices, a good conscience as he pursues a systematic critical elucidation which is always being recast and becoming increasingly radical.

Honesty is reassuring to those who find peace in having a good conscience. It guarantees nothing—except itself. This is a limited yield, and it does not ground our efforts in a solid foundation. While I consider that all modes of conduct with respect to things and ourselves (a thing among things) are unsatisfying for one or another reason, I feel that honesty is the least noxious; it blends harmoniously into the requirements we discover within ourselves, as we constantly strive to sacrifice nothing that seems essential.

Therefore, we are trying to determine that status of belief, and it is the philosopher who does this for us as he evaluates the believer's claims. When theologians affirm that theology is a science and when exegetes carry out their task in accordance with strict standards, they *ipso facto* place themselves under the philosopher's jurisdiction; exercising his role as critic, he will judge the seriousness of their work. He has not sought them out, for they are the ones to claim the rights and duties of scientific status. His task, to the degree that his philosophy is epistemological reflection, is to determine whether they measure up to the requirments of this status.

The believer claims that his discourse on a meeting with God fulfills the philosopher's requirements. Thus, the debate does not revolve around the meeting itself but around the way in which the discourse about it develops. In brief, one never judges by facts; he judges only by the way we speak about the facts and by the thoroughness and precision of our conclusions reached through them. Put in another way, truth is inexpressible. But the road we traveled to attain it can be described, and this is what we are talking about and this is what falls under the philosopher's jurisdiction. And the quality of our way of going about it, the integrity inherent in our method, will enable us to appraise what we are talking about and what we have found.

Seriousness arises when I apply my practice to a project that requires me to meet exacting standards. Seriousness is the ordering of a portion of my behavior to an aim groping toward a useful end. When what we are seeking is unclear, we are all the more convinced that seriousness resides in our way of conducting our inquiry. Even if we do not know where we are going, we can examine the mode of conduct we employ on our journey.

This is illustrated in John A. T. Robinson's book *Honest to God:* we lack the "fundamentals" for our endeavor, but we can replace them with an insistence upon honesty in our pursuit of this endeavor. Robinson sets himself the task of ridding himself of false images of God, and he finds but one sure means: "All I can do is to try to be honest—honest to God and about God—and to follow the argument wherever it leads."[28] And this honesty will lead one to the task of living in the world "even if God is not there."[29] His aim is modest; he states that he is not propounding a new model for the Church, but is merely trying to be honest, to be "open to certain 'obstinate questionings.' "[30] Thus, he finds that the believer's mode of conduct is the sole guarantee for his practice in the realm of faith. Lying beyond man's image-products and the false ideas they spawn, this guarantee is simply "conscientiousness"; for the believer and the scientist alike, applying this quality to one's methods is one of the surest means of steering clear of one's own delusions.

There is one more point which requires clarification, that is, the relationship between honesty and a good conscience. People have said a great deal about having a good conscience, and yet their talk often masks things which are dishonest. Then, too we may have misgivings about seeing honesty defined in terms of having a good conscience. Yet there is a circle here, is there not? For if we sometimes define honesty in terms of having a good conscience, at other times we define having a good conscience in terms of honesty, that is, we say that having a good conscience means being faithful to certain rules, for example, rules of operation and procedure in science. Therefore, we would do better to define good conscience in terms of honesty, not vice versa. This way we will have a clearer picture of what we want to talk about.

The open-endedness of inquiry

The question of questions concerning the believer's experience is as follows, and of all who have formulated it, Kierkegaard had done so best: "Is an historical point of departure possible for an eternal consciousness?"[31] Can the believer draw his belief from one moment in his life, a belief which envelops and determines his whole life? This is also the philosopher's question when he formulates the laws of science or reflects on the forms of laws or tries to discover the meaning of history by studying his moment in time, his epoch, or his civilization.

We cannot answer this question in the affirmative unless we realize that our Yes will be subject to doubt at a later time, in fact, subject to doubt again and again. Human truth, by nature, is a truth with a built-in awareness and acceptance that it will be challenged. It stops being a relative truth when it concedes that it is relative. Its survival as truth resides in its constantly being challenged.

The profile and totality of the religious endeavor

Life speaks to my entire being, to my mind as well as to my body, to my intellect as well as to my will and to my faculties of sense. Thus, a living enterprise should speak to my entire being too. Insofar as the philosopher and the believer are living beings, their enterprises must be considered in their totality. Many debates concerning the religious endeavor, however, speak to one's intellectual self alone. If the believer meets God, and if this believer is a living being, his meeting with God will necessarily involve his whole self. A truth which merely speaks to my intelligence is mechanical. A living truth speaks to me as to a man who want one thing and not another, who desires one thing and rejects another. And if the believer's endeavor is to be a life endeavor, it cannot engage one facet of me alone, any more than it can neglect my intellect.

Thus, a human endeavor is necesarily total, speaking to the whole man. For this reason, neither the philosopher's nor the believer's enterprise is human unless it speaks to the whole man. A human endeavor cannot be reduced to its intellectual content. Hence, the believer cannot meet God in a purely mechanical way. It is not enough that God be expressed by the intellect; he must be desired and chosen as well. This desire, as explained earlier, is born of a meeting with or an irruption of God who is not desired until he has been met and recognized.

The believer takes his form from an endeavor which calls upon his full person. The profile of the religious endeavor is worked out as follows: little by little the human imagery, the human thought-systems, fall away; some were centuries in the building, some required a certain period in an individual's life. We discover we have mystified ourselves, that we have woven the nets we are floundering in.

Man realizes he has ensnared himself the day his eyes open to the light of an Other. He realizes that he is the author of the world he is living in, that it is up to him to build the world as he will have it, that it is futile to seek solace or compensation for his ineptitude at living, for he can fashion this world to fit the life he wants to lead. A man is first of all a creature who sets out to win the world he is living in by taking it just as it is.

Without bewilderment or fear a man will be confronted by the question of an Other as he goes about his work of transforming the world. Traditions will tell him of this Other; his culture is permeated with the Other, and the most ravaged human beings are clinging to him—to God.

A man is then able to discover an affinity between his requirements and the requirements of this God his society is telling him about. We practice certain values a long time before we ask ourselves what they mean. We may find that by living the essence of what the Divine requires, without our really knowing what this is, we end up having to reply to a question which has a definite historical impact, the question Jesus of Nazareth asked Simon Peter: "Who do men say that I am, and who do you say that I am?"

"Is an historical point of departure possible for an eternal consciousness?" Kierkegaard asked.[32] We have seen that one can—first, he becomes familiar with the essence, then, he recognizes it for what it is. Exposure to divine values in historical events develops our ability to recognize God's passing by and to respond in the affirmative to Jesus of Nazareth's question. With this the believer's real history begins—with his conscious experience of God. He now strives to free himself from his own personal images, ideas, and feelings. He experienced God's essence without being able to speak of his existence. But he was not able to recognize God's passing by until the merciless criticism of the world stripped him of all that was his own. Liberated from himself, he recognized God, and doubtless his doing so could not have come about in any other way.

At this point in his history the believer turns back to things and to beings, bringing to them a strange simplicity. He rediscovers the savor of everything. Once again his life is simplified in the extreme; he has returned to the freshness and directness of childhood. Water is again water. And here he discovers that those around him are living the same history he is living and that through them he is better able to live his own. The Church becomes a communion of believers giving the same answer to the one vital question, and the sacraments become the fundamental and eternal human attitudes in harmony with the rhythm of life's phases.

We proceed, as it were, from the spontaneity of childhood to a spontaneity we rediscover through being seduced by false gods. What the believers call sin works a profound change in our consciousness. Through being misled into mythologizing and resultant bad faith, we move from a nonthetic to a thetic consciousness of God.

IMPLICATIONS

The refusal to take functions and products for values

This reflection speaks of devaluing religious practices when their conditions have specific functions to perform in a man's life, a function, for example, of an economic or psychological order. A religion is not a function. Could one go so far as to say that religion is a value?

The concept of religion is also in question; for example, in this work we are not treating Christianity as a religion, that is, in radical terms as a system of ritualistic practices which we live in our struggle toward metaphysical and ethical goals. We think of the believer's attitude in terms of an *encounter*; for us, he is the witness to a presence. At this radical level Christian belief is not a religion but, rather, actually an anti-religion, because it denies the notion that ritualistic practices determine salvation. We would say that Christian belief becomes religious in another way, that is, by spreading out into society, into the dimensions of time and space.

A possible meeting with a presence *is to no purpose*, and its very uselessness is the guarantee of its authenticity. Even if the believer is bound to receive everything from this encounter, we might say that it is just a happy accident.

God serves no purpose, and *man-made* religious constructions lead to mystification; this is one of the main points of this reflection.

When religious practices have a function to perform, they may lose their value. But how are we to define this function? How are we to define this value? We might look to Dr. Charles Odier's definitions of these terms. For him a religious practice is a function when it is "self-seeking, motivated by a conscious or unconscious will to satisfy a need or advance an individual inclination [in the general sense], without regard for social, moral, or spiritual consequences."[33] As for values, he says, "One can speak of value only when a person proposes or actually performs a step which takes him beyond the sphere of functions, beyond his biological, instinctive, and affective needs, beyond his interests in the social domain."[34] We might add that when a value is true, "all the reasons we have for seeking it, whatever they may be, are conscious in our minds."[35] The criterion will be whether or not the value is dependent on an unconsciously conceived function. I say "dependent" because a value may well have a function to perform, but not be dependent on that function. Put another way, there are probably no values in the human sphere which do not have functions associated with them; it is quite conceivable that many functions hide values. But a value becomes questionable when it is dependent on a function. Clearly, a value and a function would make an ideal combination, but the function would have to be consciously conceived, failing which it would corrupt the value. "The more elevated a value is, the higher is its position in the spiritual hierarchy and the greater the dangers it encounters."[36]

This is why it is essential to an examination of religious practices to distinguish between the elements of function and those of value, without succumbing to the temptation to reduce values to functions or to raise functions to the level of values. I take pleasure in citing Dr. Charles Odier on the analysis of religious practices: *"Anything that hampers analysis has no value!"*[37]

The necessarily social character of the believer's endeavor

This discourse begins at the level of the community. Here the witnesses speak of their testimony about a living and Other presence. They group and project their faltering descriptions toward several absolute, common certainties, such as their conviction that this living, Other presence is love.

Unless the Other is a mediator, the believer cannot proceed. It is our contention that the believer cannot be the master of this endeavor and that he cannot set himself up as the interpreter of his practices. The philosopher, as the denying mediator, furnishes the believer with the conditions necessary to the seriousness of his endeavor. This means that a person cannot discover the meaning of his practices alone. The philosopher makes quick work of the pretensions which the believer's conscience may have.

One might ask whether this confrontation between the philosopher and the believer is the consequence of strictly individual effort. Will both men have to go back over the path, each for himself? If this is what one thinks, he has not grasped the implications of the Brief Text and the commentary. The philosopher attacks a certain idea, namely, the believer's notion of God as the sedimentary deposit and given of a civilization. *As the believer thinks of God, he is inevitably engaging in a communal process, even if he is by himself.* This idea has cropped up a number of times; in fact, it is central to the problematics we described. The philosopher attacks the believer because the believer's idea of God is the product of a given society.

One might assume that the believer reacts by giving ground, surrendering God-the-product to preserve the living God to whom he is a witness, the God he has known through an experience which the philosopher cannot reduce. One might suppose that the believer is seeking his own safety as an individual and that he gives up all other claims. This is not the case. True, he surrenders God-the-product, but he is none-theless insisting on the value of his testimony about the living presence of God. Here, of course, both value and testimony must derive from a *human meeting*. The believer is telling the philosopher something like this: "The value of my testimony is contingent upon my testimony's being lived and expressed in company with my fellow believers." His discourse to the philosopher is empty unless it is the discourse of a believer belonging to the community of believers.

I have been saying that the believer's question, born of communal thought, after it has been scrutinized by the philos-opher, finally becomes a discourse whose meaning stems from its merging its voice into a discourse conducted by the be-lieving community. In other words, my prose poem and com-mentary will have been in vain if they have not put across the idea that the believer should not be thought of as an individual but as a member of a given human society. And I will now say the same of the philosopher.

The philosopher's question to the believer always arises as a step in the growth of a system of thought. This is best shown by the idea of the *change of problematics*, a key concept of this study. In the last analysis, the only questions the philos-opher raises are those which his society leads him to raise. The problematics of God was one thing before Marx and Freud came on the scene; now it is another.

Moreover, the effects of the philosopher's criticism of the believer are social in nature. His question not only modifies the social situation of the believer, but it undergoes modifica-tion itself: the philosopher is *socially* different after his ques-tion. To raise a question that is not one's own is to modify the world one is living in. The philosopher's question is as social in its development and effects as it is in its origins.

Thus, a certain idea of God is deposited in me, an idea which is the product of accumulated sedimentation, what we now call "Western civilization." I am offered a certain notion of God and am supposed to take my stand regarding testimonies about him. Many are the religious practices which proceed in this way, many the forms they take. The only way we can escape them is to put our very idea of God into question.

If I find I must call upon the concept of experience, I must be sure to do so within a framework in which others play an active role, in which they corroborate my testimony and I theirs. This will be one of the elements guaranteeing the experience; it will resemble Judaism to some extent, where "religious experience is by no means individual revelation, but communication, mutual corroboration, inquiry pursued in association with others; revelation, in the fullest sense, is necessarily interpersonal."[38]

Thus, the philosopher is summoned to a community, a necessary background, the human arena where corroboration can take place. Of course, the existence of such a community and participation in it are not a final guarantee of the seriousness of a testimony, but they must be considered a factor vital to it.

Belief, a subject fit for philosophic treatment

The philosopher has recognized his right to examine and criticize religious practice, and the believer agrees that he may do so and accepts a dialogue with regard to this process. The two men have something to say to each other. Even if it turns out that they cannot reach an understanding, they grant that an impasse is not a true reflection of their relationship unless it has been arrived at through a dialogue. If a dialogue takes them to such an impasse, they will have to break it off—on this subject, in any case. In the framework of this radical hypothesis, belief is a fit subject for philosophic treatment. This comes down to saying that the believer's discourse, for the very reason that it is a discourse, falls under the philosopher's jurisdiction.

The philosopher can only give an account of the believer's adherence to the degree that that adherence was reached through an operation in which the believer began with correct premises and then worked them through mechanically to a conclusion.[39] However, the philosopher is well within his rights when he attacks the human constructions—the idea and images—which precede, accompany, or follow this adherence. Under these conditions, a person need not be a Christian to write a philosophy of Christianity. Through the philosopher, the believer can become conscious of and deepen his religious practices. The philosopher is right to attack the believer's discourse. In fact, philosophic analysis of religious practices is an excellent mirror in which people of a given time and place can see their requirements and their state. One might even say that the merit of a given period can be assessed by the merit of its religious criticism, for such criticism allows one to determine the period's requirements, the level of its standards, its depth, and its state of consciousness.

3. CATEGORIES

A review of categories already covered in the commentary

In the commentary we discussed certain categories essential to this reflection: the categories of suspicion, of seriousness, and of concern. In the case of suspicion we wavered between two meanings—suspicion as associated with the imperceptible, and suspicion as associated with the suspect. We use the first meaning with respect to the presence of God, the second with respect to the uneasiness the philosopher and the believer feel toward a conduct which seems suspect. To avoid confusion, let us reserve the expression "to have a suspicion" for the first meaning, the expression "to suspect" for the second. We need not go back over the categories of seriousness and concern— we would only be repeating ourselves. We can now proceed to other categories, those which have not been spelled out but which are nevertheless important, the categories of the Other, of the ineffable, and of wisdom.

The Other and the ineffable

Since I could not help but consider my double as suspect, the best guarantee of the seriousness of a possible meeting with

God would be God's coming to me as an Other. I would not be meeting myself, or a projection of myself, or some hypostatized and idealized part of myself. I would be meeting an irruptive and unanticipated presence whose guarantee stems from one thing alone: from the presence's being in no way myself.

As the testimony about this presence is about the presence of an Other, I myself cannot express it, my discourse being bound to the language of my world: to express this Other would be to reduce him to myself, to betray him, and, in a sense, to deny him.

If the Other meets me, it would be easy for him to borrow the words of my world. In this case I would not be reducing him to myself; rather he would be giving himself to me. The Other, the ineffable I cannot express, can speak to me with my words. Ineffable in terms of the possible aims of my discourse, this Other is not expressed until he himself takes the initiative in speaking.

If there are words that concern God, only he can utter them. The word has no meaning with respect to him unless he is the one to speak it. Through the initiative of his word addressed to me in my language, he makes himself me. The ineffable can express himself to me, but I cannot express him. Thus, the ineffable has to make himself known to me. I cannot undertake this initiative myself. But if God does make himself known to me, perhaps it is incumbent upon me to express his word. And my word about him must be his word; otherwise, it will be nothing.

Put in another way, some form of revelation is necessary if one is to claim a right beyond that of keeping silent.

Since we are incapable of having any experience whatever without speaking about it, the ineffable is the experience of a presence which is entirely Other. This is the paradox of the man who speaks while knowing that his discourse is inane: when he keeps silent, his very silence becomes a word, for his silence stands up against other people's discourses, opposing them as the word of an Other presence. Thus, a man experiences the necessity to speak and the necessity to keep silent. His discourse leads him back to silence, and his silence is itself a discourse which he must sooner or later explain. The paradox of the ineffable is that it is expressed and that if it were not expressed, ineffability would not exist. By the same token, the experience of God is the paradox of paradoxes—*one finds it absolutely necessary to keep silent while experiencing an absolute necessity to speak.*

A witness has a paradoxical status which in itself is his guarantee: he speaks, knowing that he should not, and his intermittent silences are more expressive than his words. His discourse becomes the guarantee of his silence because his silence is the guarantee of his discourse. Thus we are always brought back to a point on this side of ourselves: every discourse is born of silence, and all silences are born of a word. The believer is always brought back to a point on this side of himself, from one trial to the next, his progress never complete, for he who is always Other is always present, and he who is always present is always Other.

To speak of God as an Other, and to persist in doing so, is to subject oneself to a strict requirement. Is this not true? A value is not true if its merit stems from the performing of a secret function. I cannot really love a person for the favors he does for me. However, in the human order, a person who does me a favor may also be a person I love. God's value is guaranteed by his being Other and by his being of no use to me. For this reason, the possibility that God will irrupt into a world where he is not anticipated offers us a greater guarantee than does the possibility that he will irrupt into a world where he is excessively anticipated and inordinately needed. In the first case, his irruption belongs to the order of value alone; in the second, it may not rise above the order of functions. Values are always consciously chosen, but this is not always true of functions.[40] A person I need and am excessively anticipating seems to be on the point of materializing everywhere, that is, I recognize him at every hand, even though he does not appear. Though I do not want to say that a value and a function cannot coincide, I must point out that value is authenticated by its being recognized, known, named, and loved while one is free from any ulterior thought that it may be useful in some way, even if one will later discover that it has the highest of uses. This is why the believer and the philosopher are both vitally interested in this theme of the irruption of an unanticipated God, a God who is of no use to us.

Wisdom

As we may distinguish between the philosopher and the sage, so may we associate the believer and the sage. The philosopher raises questions; but he always ends up asking a question he cannot answer. He is unsatisfied. Never does he bring his endeavor to completion. But the sage-believer is one who LIVES an *answer*, even if this answer is ineffable. The philosopher is never done questioning the sage-believer. And yet the sage-believer never turns away from the philosopher's question. The philosopher strips the sage-believer of his images and ideas and criticizes his endeavors. In doing this, he prepares his own death, but his death is the life of the sage-believer. The philosopher kills everything in the sage-believer which is not wisdom. The philosopher and the sage-believer can only oppose each other; they are helpless to do otherwise, but if this confrontation came to an end, the sage-believer would come to an end too. His life depends upon the philosopher's assault.[41]

4. QUESTIONS

Can we speak of a religious dimension in
Descartes' point of departure?

If we grant that experiencing the self as a thinking entity—
the Cartesian *cogito ergo sum*—can serve as the point of departure for a rigorous endeavor, can we go on to say that this
original *cogito*, taken in its full breadth, also and necessarily
contains a religious dimension? It is not my intention here to
discuss the Cartesian method. What I am asking is this: In
light of the many analyses of Descartes—for instance, Husserl's which maintains that the *cogito* brings us back face to
face with the world, with the body, and with other human
beings—can we hold that the Cartesian method, to the extent
that it is valid, necessarily raises the question of God?

I have said that there is no absolute beginning, but under
these conditions the *cogito*, while not being an absolute beginning, can nevertheless be *a* beginning, that is, be a sort
of point of crystalization for the self, albeit one which arises
after a certain time lag. In this case, can one assume that with
this beginning the question of God is already raised?

But this takes us back to an analysis of the *cogito* and to the various ways it can be interpreted. Perhaps the I of the *cogito* is not a veritable source of consciousness but merely a product of consciousness arising after a time lag. Sartre maintains that "the I which appears on the horizon of *I think* is not given as the producer of conscious spontaneity. Consciousness produces itself facing the I and goes toward it, goes to rejoin it. That is all one can say."[42] Thus, consciousness appears as an essentially impersonal phenomenon. Since we do not manage to get a sufficiently clear picture of it in its impersonality, we could say that "the *Cogito* is impure."[43]

Husserl looks to the *cogito,* taken in its breadth, for a return to the world, the body, and other human beings, without detouring through God as does Descartes. This leads one to wonder whether these horizons of selfless consciousness, that is, the *cogito,* do not necessarily imply a selfless consciousness of contingence and precariousness. And under these conditions, does not this experience which involves contingence and precariousness presuppose questions which are not thetically conscious, questions like, "Why is there being rather than nothing? Why this rather than that?" And under these conditions one might also ask whether the breadth of the *cogito* itself does not already harbor the elements of a system of religious practices. If I define such a system as selfless consciousness of a presence one can say nothing about—a presence we do not picture in images, a presence of which we have no thetic consciousness—then I might speak of "the religious dimension" of the *cogito.* But I might define this system as a set of practices followed by people who are concerned with Jesus' question to Simon Peter: "Who do you say that I am?" And one would have to say that the *cogito* contains no reference to this question. A reference of this kind presupposes a historical irruption.

Another difficulty might arise: Should the *cogito* be thought of as a reflexive operation? If the consciousness we are considering is selfless, can we talk about the possibilities of a religious dimension? Is not *self*-consciousness essential to a religious practice? Must not this practice harbor a thetic consciousness, a reflection at a second remove? Would not the religious practice arise after the appearance of the I, even if this I is a late effect in the history of the consciousness?

When I run after a streetcar, when I look at the time, when I am absorbed in contemplating a portrait, there is no *I*. . . . In fact I am then plunged into the world of objects; it is they which constitute the unity of my consciousness; it is they which present themselves with values; with attractive and repellent qualities—but *me*, I have disappeared, I have annihilated myself. There is no place for *me* on this level. And this is not a matter of chance, due to a momentary lapse of attention, but happens because of the very structure of consciousness.[44]

My point here is that religious practices may require a certain amount of elaboration and that their uniqueness no doubt lies in the fact that they cannot be pursued until one has reached a certain level of development. The truth of the matter may be that practices cannot be religious until the consciousness is gathered up to the point where it can focus upon itself. This would mean, would it not, that if the *cogito* is reflexive by nature, we might rightfully speak of its religious dimension?

Can we speak of experiencing God?

Everything seems to dovetail in such a way as to lead us to a negation of God: our experiencing evil, the burden of proof required by all the critical processes, our reflection on our own utterances about God. And yet the believer cannot abandon himself to this negation without betraying something that is essential to him; this something is an experience he has had, one which he cannot say anything about without doing it a rank injustice, one for which he could not advance a single image which a person of high standards could take seriously. Thus, the believer is a person who lives the full intensity of a negation which he cannot resign himself to—in that he wants to be true to the whole of himself; in his flesh and his heart he experiences evil and death as a negation of God. But in the name of his experience of the OTHER, he is incapable of accepting this negation. At the same time, however, he is equally incapable of yielding to this affirmation which he experiences as an ineffable encounter, unless he is willing to betray the suffering and death of others. In fact, he must be extremely modest in living this affirmation. His testimony stems from the light of his silences, and only when he acknowledges the uncertainty of his words do his words have weight.

I find that I am forced to resort to the notion of "an experience." Why do I resort to it with such reluctance? Because philosophy looks with disfavor on the idea of an experience one might have with God. Faced with the mystical experience, the philosopher holds his tongue and usually abstains from value judgements, even if he is interested in what took place. Take, for example, Baruzi's work on St. John of the Cross.

Either the mystical phenomena are treated as dynamic forces in a life in full expansion, without actually being analyzed (as Bergson did partially) or they are considered the vital forces of exoteric religions, without serious thought being given to why philosophers should take them into consideration. Put in another way, Bergson is more implicit than explicit in dealing with the most important part of the debate; in the light of what we are concerned with here, what he does not say is of greater interest than what he does say.

Therefore, what one must do is declare that this notion of experience falls within the philosopher's jurisdiction, despite what others may say. The philosopher finds that there is always something in the believer's system of practices that cannot be reduced: the experiencing of a presence which has been gradually emptied of all content susceptible to representative expression, either sensible or intellectual. The believer affirms that God is there, that he knows he is there, even though the philosopher has deprived him of all his images, ideas, and feelings of God. If we assume that the believer is an honest man, we find that as the dialogue between him and the philosopher develops, the believer soon has nothing left, at least nothing which he feels stands up under the philosopher's criticisms—yet the believer is bound to continue to affirm this presence of God, even though it has been emptied of everything which might express it, even though it has sustained every criticism the philosopher could bring to bear. Thus, we continue to speak of someone, and we do so on the ravaged horizon of our extinguished dreams, a someone we can now say nothing about. This is the believer's paradox. And finally, it is this paradox which causes the philosopher to see the believer as a serious person. Through being stripped of everything, yet continuing to exist, the believer becomes a witness in the philosopher's eyes.

Thus, the mystical experience should be integrated into the philosopher's field of study. In fact, it may be the metaphysician's prime concern. There is more than one way to bring this about.

There is integration under duress and there is integration betokening victory. The first is the process of the philosopher who, after many refusals and critical steps, finally realizes that, in spite of everything, he has to recognize the believer. Here integration comes about in terms of dialogue. In victorious integration, the believer becomes a philosopher who knows the wonderful richness of the mystical experience and who considers it the core of all metaphysical discourses; because of this he has no great esteem for the philosopher's journey. He looks down on the philosopher's hesitant advances, his backtracking, the concessions he makes, his regrets about his earlier skepticism, his final recognition which almost seems to be obtained through extortion. Victorious integration takes place, as if by *magic*, at an absolute point of view, without pausing for the hesitation of others or for refusals encountered along the way. It proceeds rather too much as though man is God, and thereby it slips away from its purpose—that of introducing the believer's experience into the philosopher's field of study. But this means forgetting that philosophy is a human endeavor and that the philosophies which claim to locate themselves at the level of the absolute and to push off from there may no longer be philosophies at all: such philosophies assume that God has been reached, possessed, and developed by human discourses; they affirm the value of the mystical point of view, without any sensitivity for the philosopher's doubts. Victorious integration presents us with a believer who has banished doubt, with a man who has lost patience with the waverings of the philosopher, considering them useless meanderings and wasted time. To me this is somewhat the attitude of Morel in his *Le Sense de L'Existence selon Saint Jean de la Croix* (the Introduction to Volume I in particular). We will give lengthy consideration to Morel's effort to integrate the mystical experience into the philosopher's meditations.

If we want to make a place for this experience in our reflection, we must determine its value and the way it fits into our study. Baruzi writes at the close of his book on St. John of the Cross, "doubtless there is no reason why one cannot, through the rhythm of the metaphysical effort, transpose the bitter purification of the spirit."[45] A remark of this sort leads one to think that there may be a parallel between the mystical experience and metaphysics. But in the second edition of his work Baruzi speaks out against an interpretation of this kind. "It never entered my mind—as certain people thought in strangely misreading the closing lines of this work—to 'transpose' a mystical experience into metaphysical inquiry by means of a systematic decision.[46] For Baruzi, "Mysticism is not a close world which superposes itself on any sort of pre-mystical thought-system."[47] And one could conceive of making "a metaphysics out of mysticism. But it would have nothing to do with a philosophic *quest.*"[48]

In other words, mysticism and philosophy seem to relate in the following way: the mystical endeavor and philosophic inquiry *do not resemble each other at all,* are not even parallel pursuits, but the philosopher can try to decipher a metaphysical meaning in the mystical process. Philosophy seems to be capable of interpreting the mystical endeavor without going so far as to claim that it explains it or that it validates or invalidates it; the mystical process can be studied from this point of view, just as it can be studied by psychology. Baruzi says that "the doctrine of St. John of the Cross is enormously helpful to us *considering the problem of mysticism from a metaphysical point of view.*"[49] Thus, the problem is one of knowing how mystical experience—or, by the same token, theology—relates to metaphysics. For there is an entire theology which does not account for the mystical experience, but merely mentions it as an element exterior to its principles and development. It seems that, in general, metaphysics and philosophy have inherited from classical theology a profound mistrust for those who have recourse to the mystical experience; it is enough, evidently, to call to mind the strong suspicions brought to bear on John of the Cross and Theresa of Avila, who were taken for the Alumbrados visionaries.[50] However, we should note that St. Theresa herself had recourse to an experiential criterion in determining the value of her evidently supernatural visions and utterances.[51]

Be it said that the notion of mystical experience can be thought of in other ways too. It is not limited to being the source or fulcrum for the believer's endeavor; it can be an enrichment of faith: "This God in whom St. John of the Cross rediscovers the world is reached beyond things and beyond images."[52] And the experience leads the believer to live like "a man whose theopathic life seems to culminate in new perception of things, to culminate in the world's essence penetrating into God, to culminate in a sort of experience of infinite attributes."[53]

Morel begins by harking back to Baruzi's thesis: mysticism bears no relationship to metaphysics. For Baruzi, according to Morel, mysticism and metaphysics relate to different levels and endeavors of the spirit; Morel does not agree. For Baruzi, again according to Morel, the philosopher can only follow his hero to a certain point: he can understand him, observe him, love him, but he himself cannot take part. The philosopher can live *within himself* what the mystic lives *outside of himself*. This is how Morel sums up Baruzi's position.

For Morel, the religious experience is not founded through purely *a priori* or *a posteriori* methods "for it has its source in the reality which transcends these two, and which in founding them gives them their meaning."[54] Morel finds fault with the Husserlian type of philosophy because of its total inability to move out of the category of consciousness; he takes this opportunity to retrace the Cartesian, Spinozist, and Hegelian schemata. To avoid doubt, Descartes draws in zone by zone to a center which he considers impregnable—the *I*.[55] Spinoza runs into the same doubt, but for him the impregnable center is God. This marks the beginning of the history of nostalgia for the absolute which we will encounter later in Kant. The essential problem centers on the relationship between religion and philosophy, and Hegel feels that on this point his contemporaries wear themselves out in sterile debate. The world has been cut into two pieces, and the task at hand is to restore it to its wholeness.

There is kinship, Morel explains, between the thought of Hegel and Kant. Why does Hegel take a stand against Spinoza? Spinoza sees that negation lies at the heart of things. But this he merely sees. His philosophy is worked out from a contemplative point of view. For Hegel, negation can only be grasped as a *movement*. "Negation is not real unless it is felt."[56] It cannot be described from without.

Morel raises the question "Is there really a double path— metaphysics and mysticism—leading to the real?"[57] The return to daily life desired by his contemporaries seems to be purchased at the expense of "total renunciation of nostalgia for the absolute."[58] And Morel cites Merleau-Ponty as an example of this attitude. Morel refers to an article entitled "Sens et Non-Sens," which Merleau-Ponty wrote, and attempts to point out the difficulties which Merleau-Ponty has fallen into.

Morel claims to oppose these points of view with an "experience of the absolute" which begins with life "in this world."[59] He wants to point out a road of "reconciliation" for those who are weary of "wavering."[60] According to Morel, God is not a concept but a "presence which establishes and transfigures all concepts."[61] For Morel, St. John of the Cross opens a "royal highway toward the domain of reality to which all metaphysicians aspire."[62]

This point of view raises some questions. The validity of the mystical experience is postulated implicitly in such a manner —and with faith, no doubt, as its point of departure—that we have the believer imposing it upon the philosopher. This option becomes, in Morel's eyes, the condition which makes metaphysics possible. Must one not conclude from this that the act of faith is a prerequisite to a serious pursuit of metaphysics and that without this act of faith the philosopher is more or less bound to err? Therefore, this position is very dogmatic; basically, it refuses any dialogue with those who believe it impossible to validate this type of experience philosophically, and it may remove the mystical experience from the philosopher's jurisdiction.

Now then, critical reflection is not incapable of making important contributions to the mystical endeavor. Accordingly, the philosopher no longer considers mysticism a foreign field of study; for him, mysticism becomes a road leading to the real and is unchallengeable philosophically for reasons which have been placed out of his reach. Those who are not willing to approach the problem in this way are *ipso facto* more or less disqualified from philosophic pursuits. This leads to a certain intolerance. In essence, Morel points to the believer-mystic as a proprietor of the truth, and says that philosophy, through failing to accept this truth, has been straying hither and yon for several centuries. I wonder whether Morel is not offering us an excessively "victorious" analysis of the mystical experience, one which might even constitute a sort of *naturalization of mysticism*. What he is saying is that unless one begins with mysticism, metaphysics is out of the question.

Therefore, if we have recourse to the idea of an experience, we must spell out the impact of the experience. Our task here has been to analyze the dialogue between the philosopher and the believer. If we speak of the possibility of a person's experiencing God, that person is necessarily a *believer,* not a random individual who has not yet had occasion to reply affirmatively to the question God puts to him. This affirmative reply alone enables the believer to speak of his experience. To experience the presence of God means to have recognized God at an earlier point in time. Basically, the schema which is the least suspect maintains that one is nourished by God's essence for a long time, that is, one is nourished for a long time by God's values, his life, and his spirit, without in any way experiencing him or being conscious of him; then God asks his question, and if we recognize who he is, we become able to experience his presence. Using the vocabulary of phenomenology, we might go so far as to say that the step from nonthetic to thetic consciousness of God is taken through the *question of God*. We might go still further and say that the step from experiencing God's essence to experiencing his presence is taken through the mediation of language, in a dialogue in which God takes the initiative.

What I have just said tends to reject the idea that the experience we have of God is some sort of direct intuitive knowledge of him; this knowledge would merely be a new human product replacing the images, ideas, and feelings we tried to do away with. *A new product should not step in to become man's experience of God;* the experience can only result from an irruption of God, from a sort of response man makes to the presence of God, recognized now through the believer's adherence. In short, let us say that the experience does not form the basis for adherence but that adherence makes the experience possible.

God keeps silent. Perhaps the reason for this is simply that he is absent, that he does not exist. But a man trying desperately to make him exist will try to justify God's silence. He will come up with all kinds of theories, even a theory of silence, and thus silence will become the word, and everything is to be found in everything, and we find our way back to God, and everybody is happy. But this is a big farce, is it not? So, proofs do not work? Then let us forget proof; let us be witnesses to an experience of God. But does experience command more authority than proof? Is it not a proof in disguise? Something we do not want to see reduced to a proof but is one just the same? Having felt we were obliged to turn to experience, we now find ourselves wavering between two temptations: the temptation to reject experience in that it seems to elude anyone who wants to verify it and the temptation to embrace illuminism, that is, to consider the way clear to all sorts of flights of fantasy, invented by a mind seeking consolation. Therefore, the experience of God is a private matter which we live while menaced from two quarters: we are threatened, on the one hand, by our own tendency to refuse the experience through our desire for rationality and proof; we are threatened, on the other, by our tendency toward exultation, which is merely a naive and immediate trust in the subtleties of our imagination.

We find that we have to turn to this experience, even though we have no guidelines to keep us from these dangers.

We must live this experience without clearly defined signposts to indicate the path. If we could draw up a list of measures which we could follow to keep from losing the way, the problems raised in this book would be solved; but the philosopher admits that he is unable to offer the believer any such safeguards, just as the believer himself is unable to draw up any sort of list. And to the believer the philosopher is like Socrates' devil who told Socrates what he should not do but never what he should do. Because of this, the believer's experience becomes the reason, subject matter, and framework for exchanges with other men, and the soundest evaluations of this experience will be made at the level of these exchanges. It is clear that recourse to this experience is not enough to allow a person to state his position to others. The experience can be authenticated by God alone; as we said earlier, God alone can put the question of God to man in a serious manner.

Conclusions

"THIS work has made it difficult to become a Christian, so difficult that among people of culture in Christendom the number of Christians will perhaps not be very great. I say 'perhaps' for I can have no certain knowledge of such things."[63] It is difficult to ask oneself the question of God in a serious way. If one thinks about it, he always finds he has not asked it with enough seriousness, and again and again he goes back to the beginning to start afresh. However, this is a good sign. In fact, it is the only good sign there is. Is it possible that Christians must decrease in number in order to increase? Yes; in fact, it is undeniable, and the Christian must wane to the point of being denied, of being crushed and subjugated, in order to truly rise again as the authentic witness of a living, moving presence. This is terrifying. This statement could well lead to enmity among the shepherds of the greater flock. But Dostoyevski's Grand Inquisitor is a shepherd of the greater flock, so much so that he finds he must turn away from Christ. It may not be right that a shepherd of the greater flock should make being a Christian a simple matter. The time has come when the more one says, the more clearly one indicates that to be a Christian is difficult, and the more people feel that this

137

is a good sign. God has been made such an easy matter that we have put ourselves in his place. Marx and Freud did a good thing in demythologizing that particular god. Only the person whose testimony refers to himself need fear being demythologized. If God is really an Other, why should one fear? The man of God is either the witness to an Other, or merely the witness to himself, in other words, to NOTHING which has value now.

All this is quite simple. But simplicity is exacting, and the world learns to be exacting as it becomes adult.

There is NOTHING left; but only when one begins with NOTHING, can one construct something in a serious way. For man, like God, is a product of man. And my humanist requirements, far from being a source of my values, should be thought of as the fruit of a history.

In any case, one thing is clear: man is not the oldest or most important problem human knowledge has had to deal with. Let us take a relatively short time span and a limited geographic area— European culture since the seventeenth century. We can be sure that in this background man is a very recent invention. The archeology of our thought easily proves that man is a recent invention, and possibly one which will soon fall by the wayside.

If these structures were to disappear in the way they appeared, if— through some sort of event which we might be able to imagine but whose form or consequences we cannot predict—they were to totter, as did the foundations of classical thought at the turn of the eighteenth century, then we can wager that man would vanish by his own hand, washed away like a face in the sand.[64]

The way in which I define myself as a human being is a product of the society I am living in. It has taken us several

centuries to work out this definition. And this definition produces me in turn, with my questions, just as it produces the
questions I put to myself. The question of God is only one
among countless others. All of them have a hand in producing
me. If these products we produce disintegrate, then other horizons may come into view.

That which is really only myself I refuse to consider *other*.
I reject God to the extent that I find him my creation or the
product of the society I am living in. If I ask myself whether
God can be something other than this product, I am still not
playing fair, because this question is my attempt to save the
product I need for stabilizing the world I live in. Therefore,
if I want to be thorough and precise, I cannot question myself
about God.

And I do want to be thorough and precise. If I question
myself, my questioning is limited to my practices, to my asking
myself whether my practices are thorough and precise with
respect to this *other;* this *other* is the presence I cannot express
in my discourse but which I nevertheless affirm. The question
merely concerns the experience of irruptive expressions of
otherness as they give rise to these discourses I am asking myself about. From this standpoint alone can we give serious consideration to those people who claim to be talking about God
in a serious manner.

There is nothing left, and everything is fair game for the
demythologization process. To exempt oneself from a given
form of criticism means to refuse to try to make a practice a
serious matter. Paraphrasing Francis Jeanson in support of my
main contention, I maintain that there is no such thing as a
select Christian practice distinct from pagan practices; all there
are are human practices of lesser and greater degrees of iso-

lation, all of which claim to possess concretized and deified values and ideals. There is a practice which is simultaneously a requirement; it exists and does not exist, it must be created and is struggling every day to materialize, that is, it is struggling to produce a man who is not the mystified product of his own making.[65]

In these pages we are expressing our refusal to be mystified by God-the-product. Our idea of God is the product of a civilization, of a type of society; we will have to strip ourselves of that idea in order to create the conditions for seriousness. But we will be merely simplifying questions if we are really exacting only with our idea of God. As I have said, our idea of man is also the product of a world. Now then, God is reduced in the name of an idea of man. Our will to reach a self-consistent whole and our demand for seriousness are only understandable when they proceed from our most basic experiences. All discourses are about the experience, and error is one of the forms of the experience: error does not begin until it is experienced.

Therefore, the task is to create conditions favorable to a serious religious practice. But doing this inevitably leads to confusion. On the one hand, we want to quell our expectations, to learn to anticipate nothing at all, for expectations secrete the very things they expect to encounter; but, on the other, we say that as we live in this desert, anticipating nothing at all, something steps forward which we have not produced. We think that "it is bound to step forward sometime," and is this not a new form of anticipation?

There is no way out of this confusion. The religious man is doomed to trust what may step forth and yet to have skeptical reserve for what actually appears. One steps beyond this confusion, however, through adherence, through one's religious practice, and in so doing, points to an irreducible experience which will establish the religious man's discourse.

If we open the door to experience, if we turn our attention to what everyone is experiencing, would we not be closing the door to seriousness? If we turn to everyman's experience, as turn we must, how can me make this step serious? This very question marks the social character of the step: "Sense . . . is revealed where the paths of my various experiences intersect, and also where my own and other people's intersect and engage each other like gears."[66] To us, this verification—this activity in which we bring certain moments of ourselves into contact with other moments of ourselves and with what other people are experiencing—is a valuable step in the pursuit of seriousness.

Recourse to experience would also mean that "the world is not what I think but rather what I live."[67] Throughout this book I have been talking about a refusal to reduce the real to a certain idea of the world, hence to something which is a product. Our task is to sink our roots into the real, and as we proceed with our theoretic thought we must constantly bear in mind that "we produce the products which produce us."[68] There is only one area in which all our endeavors can take serious root, and that is in what we are experiencing. The difficulty is to be aware of this, to be thorough and precise in assessing whether our endeavors are actually rooted there, and to realize that our assessment is forever bound to be incomplete.

This theme of ours is nothing new. In the seventeenth century Brother Lawrence of the Resurrection, alias Nicholas

Herman, centered his spirituality on the experiencing of God's presence.[69] But what is new here is the integration of this experience into philosophic discourses on religious practice—no one has succeeded in doing this to date. I have tried to stress that this experience is the only sound foundation for a religious discourse and that, without it, such a discourse will not meet the test of seriousness. The real problem is to determine whether a religious discourse has sunk its roots into life itself and taken hold there; at the same time, one will determine whether the discourse is not merely the product of images and concepts which the person has created to make sense out of his experience.

We have also seen that the religious man's discourse cannot wind up in a fruitful conclusion. He speaks so that he may say that he cannot help but speak about something that is happening; he is also speaking to tell us there is NOTHING he can say. An OTHER is the only one who can speak; in fact, the religious man can only speak to the degree that his discourse is the discourse of this OTHER. Now then, the discourse of the OTHER is couched in the language of the man who has just said he can say nothing. This leads to great confusion because the danger of mythmaking is enormously increased. The scope of this demythologization process cannot help but terrify the traditional believer.

For this process will spare NOTHING, not the Church, not images of God, not the Christian discourse which has come down through the centuries, not the dogmas and their diverse formulations. The Christian must submit to the test or be disqualified. All too often the desire to side-step things has caused Christians to fall into mythmaking.

There is a cause for alarm here for the traditional believer:

are there no limits to the scope of this criticism? Is there not a certain body of revealed truths, a stock of traditions consecrated by years of Christian life, which need not fall prey to this scrutiny? I will not go into the contradictions at play in a reaction of this sort, nor will I discuss its failure to offer us a serious theory of the relationship between philosophy and theology. I will merely indicate its source—fear. Fear of everything: fear of watching a world crumble; fear of seeing the values of this world vanish—this stems from confusing *a* world with *the* world; fear of man himself, such fear that one reaches the point where he cannot trust anyone, where he will not risk anything whatever for anyone at all; fear of oneself, such fear that one no longer understands that he must blaze his own trail, that he must stop acting like an automaton, that he must stop following the meanderings of destinies like those pre-established by horoscopes; fear of God whose image has gradually assumed all the features of oppression. Truly, the motor nerve of all integrisms is fear.

This very fear is nothing more or less than a sign of weak faith. What does a Christian have to fear at the level of his faith? What are the critical attacks he must dread? What kind of analysis will ever be capable of reducing the authentic elements in his practice?

"Anything that is damaged by analysis is without value."[70] Indeed, a thing of true value has nothing to lose in the hands of analysis and criticism in any form. Is a believer not suspect if he refuses analysis and criticism which put his practices into question? Is his fear not a sign that he himself feels he may have fallen into mythmaking?

Believers, accustomed to the comforts of a world they think

they are living in, refuse to see the products which produce us put into question: many are the formulas, many the forms, ideas, and habits, which they *defend*. They fear an attempt on God's life. But he has already been killed by the philosophers. Terrified by the sacrilegious, blasphemous attacks of philosophy, the believers defend themselves by becoming rigid and intransigent—in their eyes, this is the only way they can safeguard their religious practices. God died in the last century; we gradually realize that the God who died was not God. Attempts are made to deny that he is dead, but on examining the body we find that the body does not belong to a God. The terrified are the only ones who will not come forward to see who it is that died.

Yes, God is dead. And through this death alone does he live. This is the final word in what I have been trying to say. The dead things with which people want to weight down the living merely burden religious endeavors to the point of bringing them to a halt. This is true at all levels, in and outside the Churches. This is widely known.

However, the greater flock still has the idea that the transition from death to life ought to be dealt with in steps: one must not rush this mutation; people must be given time. But time for what exactly, if not for covering living things over with dead things so that life is not too . . . lively?

Thus, I have divested myself of an absolute which was merely a product. Would I dare to make the claim that I myself have discovered myself? No, for this would mean considering myself free from all mythmaking; it would mean secretly reintroducing the absolute which I have rid myself of. No, here I am, poor, helpless, existing by chance in this

time and place, surrounded by other men. And we have a
world to build. Setting up the absolute is not within my
powers. I am asked, "What are you doing to your faith, to the
Church, to Jesus Christ?" To this I reply that I broach only
those questions Jesus Christ puts to me, in other words, broach
only those questions which I cannot ask myself. The Churches
bring people together who take these questions seriously, and
this is what faith represents first and foremost—these communities, these gatherings of people who consider the questions
Christ raises a serious matter.

Moreover, there is not a single question that I can exempt
from critical study. This is the *philosophic* condition of my
religious endeavor. The modern sciences owe their development to their ability to clear up misunderstandings, and
NOTHING we can point to is immune to misunderstanding.
No religious practice, in fact, no practice of any kind, can be
serious if it will not allow itself to be analyzed. Doubtless, a
time of greater seriousness is coming; analysis will be the first
step in every important engagement, and those who refuse to
analyze will be disqualified. We can expect mankind of the
future to have an increasingly clear understanding of its op-
tions, engagements, and practices, so that it will never be the
plaything of its products. The time has come when neurotic
practices with their false security can be sorted out from other
very authentic things, and at times this can be actually done
on this side of neurosis.

Is there some hope that we may rediscover our fundamental
projects here on this side of mythmaking influences, rediscover
them intact and beyond suspicion here on this side of all that
conditions us, on this side of these societies we live in and

lose ourselves in, here where God does not exist? Let us not forget that we *become* Christians and that we encounter Christ and our fellowman. Anything else that happens is necessarily accidental. In short, we must rediscover what our products really are—merely products; this is the way we may go on intact to our projects, carrying them into that area where everything favors our not being mystified.

People have wanted to silence these dangerous people who put everything back into question. But when those who disparage dangerous people do this, they silence themselves and perform a useful act. For times have changed. The Gods who were defended in all those citadels are dead Gods. The goal was to free the living from battles that were not worth fighting. Enormous energy was mobilized, but what was being defended? Dismantled structures whose parts were still being cleaned and maintenanced. Alas, many groaned at being assigned this task. They suffered while they lived and thought, and no small few had to die forsaken, to die for a life which apparently had no sense. Let us be fair: we are harvesting the fruit of their sacrifice; we are indebted to them for our being able to live today with more light and air.

But this is a life without illusions. As we explain the healthy requirements for a sound religious practice, our greatest danger is that we will be misunderstood. We will be attacked with texts cited out of context and distorted by the use they are put to; this is because we maintain and believe that we are living in an age following Marx, Freud,[71] and Einstein, and that all endeavors must be rooted in this awareness, failing which, they will lack seriousness. How much easier it would be to keep silent.

New forces have come into play. The Christian world is awakening. Public opinion concerns the Churches now. Questions are being asked. Gone are the days when a voice raised in opposition could be stifled; it used to begin with a start of alarm, an investigation, some sort of decree scarcely noticed for the most part and possibly not even made known to those involved. Thus, they were stifled without being properly heard; then they were forsaken, broken in this echoless world of silence, obscurity, or lack of comprehension.

Today, in a more enlightened world, the choices are simplified. The dilemma is clear: either a total effort will be made to make religious practices serious—with all forms of analytical or critical investigation being welcome, be they act or word—or believers will cease being heard and will snuff themselves out on the candelabra.

Christians who are frightened accuse the world of turning a deaf ear to the message of the gospel; rarely do they take the blame on themselves. If the world found Christians less mystified, it might be more attentive to their testimony!

But things take a curious turn, and those who are frightened ought to take comfort here; the enormous interest which has developed in the *historical* orgins of our religious practices draws attention to the debates about the history of Jesus and brings these debates into the foreground. The demythologization process we have discussed, when extended in scope, encourages people to turn back to the sciences that deal—some directly, some indirectly—with the Holy Scriptures. The integrist sclerosis sooner or later leads one to mistrust history and gradually decreases the possibility of a meeting with Christ. On the other hand, demythologization, through its demands, expands research into history and linguistics and defines our meeting with Christ. Concern with historocity destroys many things but leads to solid foundations. Conceptual rigidity, through distrust of history, brings about its own destruction.

Analysis can degenerate into petty debate, into attacks on the general tendencies of a point of view; but when handled properly, the will to analyze a practice is, as a condition of the validity of this practice, necessary and unimpeachable.

This necessity applied now to our vital concern—to our moving toward a living question—leaves us in a universe which is stripped bare and is possibly even ravaged. Yesterday's world gave meaning to certain problems, for example, discussions about the demonstrability of the existence of God. But the meaning of these problems was secreted by yesterday's world—a world which was well-defined, namely, the West with its Christian culture, which was dominated by Roman Catholic dogmatics. The world has changed, as have the problems, and the meaning given these problems is merely counterfeit species in a new and different world. This meaning was a *verbal* solution to life problems secreted by a particular world. Our concepts help us to solve our problems, but we are mystified because our problems are not properly *ours:* they emerge from the structures of the civilization we live in. Everything is already set up, already organized: a given society lives on its own tensions—strong tensions in our Western world—and these tensions give rise to life problems. We solve them with a system of concepts, a pattern of the world, a ready-made network of ideas and relationships, and this system becomes the matrix of our discourse. It does not come from us but is a discourse belonging to the world we live in, one which already existed, intact, before we as individuals came on the scene. Words help us to cope with the world's tensions.

The "problem of the existence of God" and the various solutions offered in answer to it was a problem of this sort; it was the product of a world. At the beginning the question "Does God exist?" was not properly and personally our own; it was the ready-made question secreted by the problems of the world our parents lived in. One must put many miles behind himself and be uprooted time and time again—probably a thing very few could bear—before he can make such a question personal.

Since we have nothing to say that originates in us, since when we speak, something else is always speaking in our place, the nothing we have come to can be regarded as a provisional but honest point of departure: provisional, in that we may one day discover that even this *nothing* has been produced by something other than ourselves, something which has been on the scene all along, and our requirements will force us to take a further step back; honest in that, provisionally, it is the purest, the most stripped down, the most original and the least suspect thing I have found.

"Our" old concepts—and the reason for my quotation marks is clear—"our" problems of yesterday nevertheless enabled us to realize we were mystified, enabled us to draw in the boundaries of what produces us, enabled us to make our way toward fundamental attitudes of life, enabled us to spell out these attitudes when we might have been content to take our products for radical beginnings.

However, even if we become more exacting and less mystified, we still live in a systematized world which lives on tensions, which secretes products, concepts, questions, etc., which uses words and discourses to solve the life problems it cannot deal with in a successful way. If we become aware of what enchains us, we have a chance to increase the seriousness of our religious practices.

We are talking here about a debate one carries on with oneself; but on closer look it turns out that there is no debate with oneself. The only questions one raises are those which a given culture at a given time leads one to raise. Whenever one of us carries on a debate with himself, the questions he raises are not chosen at will; they are brought up by something other than himself, something preexistent, a given. It is interesting to note the particular questions raised, to observe that they are not random or arbitrary. This is why my questions and my debates are not actually *mine*. My doubts are of no great importance in and of themselves; they are important for what they reveal, and this that they reveal does not stem from me. They reveal the manner in which a certain discourse on God reaches me as it encounters questions raised by a certain moment in—or state of—the culture I live in.

The individual debates and questions also direct us to something that lies on this side of the individual, to something which explains why these are the particular debates and questions raised. All efforts which are reflexive, that is, which are introspective in the narcissistic sense of the term, urge us to seek something on this side of the individual, a something which quickens the debates and questions of Narcissus himself. To our moralizing analysts, the world of Narcissus is a maze without an exit, a closed universe which ends up in the death of self-contemplation; yet to our eyes, Narcissus is only possible when a certain language and a certain culture lives in and organizes itself in a certain discourse which brings Narcissus into being.

Therefore, the important thing here is not to determine whether the debate is taking place within the believer, in terms of reason and faith, but to discover how a debate of this kind originally became possible. When we analyzed the conditions of this debate, we explained the radical requirements which must envelop—or, if one prefers, circumscribe—the discourse by which the debate is carried on. Any debate, however individualized it may be, is of great and general interest the moment it adopts a second line of inquiry—one which tries to establish why this individual is asking himself this particular question instead of that. Our question of God is no exception.

For both reason and faith have a history: born of mutations of language, they contributed to new mutations in turn. The thought-systems which made them possible were themselves transformed by these irruptions. Every human question belongs to a certain time and place; until we accept the idea that nothing, not even God, escapes the historicity of our discourses, we cannot get closer to what is actually being experienced—and this goes for what we experience in our religious practices too.

I set forth with the Prose Poem, my unsophisticated point of departure, then continued on through my commentary and my subsequent reflection on this commentary, and these are the conclusions I have reached. To my mind the venture has been well worth the effort; possibly it has defined the conditions one could assign to the contemporary religious dialogue.

As the reader reaches the end of this meditation, he may want to know something about my own relationship to the Church. I will not disappoint him.

First, I would like to point out that one enters the Church, that one comes to it—even if it comes toward us. But since one comes to it, one is already someone, one already belongs to a world. And before saying what the Church has given me, I must point out that every human being who comes to it, brings something to it. Today's world, through those who move toward the Church, brings forth new requirements born of new social structures. No one can prevent this from happening. No one can deny that the social structures of the world are what they are, and this is basic to our thought. The Church reviews its thinking with regard to what the world as it is is thinking. Therefore, we can say that in the Church every human being is a witness to a world, and everyone should be accepted in this role.

Now then, the Church has stiffened all my requirements. The social world of the Church has not opposed my vital thought—far from it—but has stimulated it. The Church is the living melting pot where I sometimes take form against my findings. Things lead me to act and to think my actions through. Since the Church itself is a historical reality, it is the source of tensions which are the condition of life in our form of society. The Church cannot play a conservative role, for it is not a homogeneous monolith, but a diversified social structure. The tensions arising among diversified groups in the Church are a source of life, a wellspring of thought and action. In this book I have spent my life forces in order to combat everything that is dead: things, ideas, questions, problems, at times even men. Since my life forces have been restored, why should I adore a dead God? The Church itself has raised and stiffened all the requirements I bring to practices which I want to be religious. I am not formed through opposition to the Church; I am formed by the Church.

These remarks and admissions stem from a question of utmost importance to my subject: Without the Church, would my requirements concerning religious practices have ever come to light? Would they merely have died? For these requirements, like all discourses, concepts, problems, and questions, are not my own: they are the action of a world which exists before I come onto the scene, a world in which I awaken, where I take my form. These requirements arise from a social world which produces me in the matrix of its language. This adds new weight to the point I have been trying to make: if I live these requirements, I necessarily do so through the Church in which I am taking form. These requirements are not original with me but are merely the product of the world I live in, a preexistent world, one in which the Church has sunk its roots. If I am allowed to live and to pursue these requirements rising from a multiform world, I do so through the Church which produces me and offers me freedom. Nothing can be built and nothing can be embraced until one has accepted, ceased to suffer from, and exorcised the fear of having nothing left.

FOOTNOTES

1. As the term "category" has a number of meanings, I should specify that here I am using it to mean a point of crystallization of my thoughts in a given area of study.

2. In *The World and the West* Arnold J. Toynbee explains why "World" comes before "West" in the title: "This title, as it stands, was chosen deliberately, in order to make two points that seem essential for an understanding of the subject. The first point is that the West has never been all of the world that matters. The West has not been the only actor on the stage of modern history even at the peak of the West's power (and this peak has perhaps now already been passed). The second point is this. In the encounter between the world and the West that has been going on by now for four or five hundred years, the world, not the West, is the party that, up to now, has had the significant experience. It has not been the West that has been hit by the world; it is the world that has been hit—and hit hard—by the West; and that is why, in the title of this book, the world has been put first . . . for us Westerners, it is today still a strange experience to be suffering at the hands of the world what the world has been suffering at Western hands for a number of centuries past." *The World and the West* (New York: Oxford University Press, 1953), pp. 1, 2, and 4.

3. Søren Kierkegaard, *Concluding Unscientific Postscript*, trans. by David F. Swenson and Walter Lowrie (Princeton: Princeton University Press, 1941), p. 28.

4. I have a reason for specifying *personal* beings, for when Rayleigh

and Ramsey did their painstaking work toward discovering argon, they were first acquainted with many aspects or argon, that is, they knew what it was, they knew its essence before they established that it was existent, that is, before they isolated it as a new gas and gave it a name.

5. Karl Barth, *Anselm: Fides Quaerens Intellectum,* trans. by Ian W. Robertson (Richmond: John Knox, 1960), p. 61.

6. *Ibid.,* p. 74.

7. *Ibid.,* p. 171.

8. Kierkegaard, *Concluding Unscientific Postscript, op. cit.,* p. 407: "The uncertainty is the criterion, and the certainty without the uncertainty is the criterion for the absence of a God-relationship."

9. John A. T. Robinson, *Honest to God* (Philadelphia: Westminster, 1963), p. 124.

10. *Ibid.,* p. 126.

11. See Kierkegaard, *Concluding Unscientific Postscript, op. cit.,* p. 438: "Dialectics itself does not see the absolute, but it leads, as it were, the individual up to it, and says: 'Here it must be, that I guarantee; when you worship here, you worship God.' But worship itself is dialectics."

12. Bachelard, in *La Philosophie du Non,* examines the evolution of the concept of mass and establishes that reason's priority over reality is one of the characteristics of the new scientific spirit. Today we are living in a world where reason moves faster than images, and images are becoming an obstacle to the observance of exacting standards.

13. See Amédée Ayfre's book, *Conversion aux Images?* (Paris: Éditions du Cerf), pp. 7-16.

14. Dumery, *Phénoménologie et Religion* (P. U. F.), p. 11.

15. Kierkegaard, *Concluding Unscientific Postscript, op. cit.,* p. 275.

16. In Louis Althusser's book *Pour Marx,* which is a study of Marx's relationship to Hegel (Éditions Maspéro), we have a fine example of the richness of the concept of *problematics* and the infinitely productive use one can put it to. See p. 63, and especially pp. 59-83 for more detailed treatment.

17. First Vatican Council, 1870, the Dogmatic Constitution on the

Catholic Faith; see Dumeige, *La Foi catholique* (Éditions de l'Orante, No. 86), p. 69.

18. Anti-Modernist oath (1910); see Dumeige, *ibid.*, No. 126, p. 80.

19. See *L'Éternité dans la Vie Quotidienne*, (Bruges: Desclée De Brouwer), pp. 136-138.

20. Merleau-Ponty, *Phenomenology of Perception*, trans. by C. Smith (New York: Humanities, 1962), p. 56.

21. Karl Barth, *Anselm: Fides Quaerens Intellectum, op. cit.*, p. 38: "*Nec quaerete re possum, nisi tu doceas, nec invenire, nisi te ostendas.*"

22. *Ibid.*, pp. 37-38.

23. See St. John of the Cross, *The Ascent of Mount Carmel*, Book I, Chapter XIII:

> To reach satisfaction in all
> desire its possession in nothing.
>
> To come to the knowledge of all
> desire the knowledge of nothing.
>
> To come to possess all
> desire the possession of nothing.
>
> To arrive at being all
> desire to be nothing.
>
> To come to the pleasure you have not
> you must go by a way in which you enjoy not.
>
> To come to the knowledge you have not
> you must go by a way in which you know not.
>
> To come to the possession you have not
> you must go by a way in which you possess not.

To come to be what you are not
you must go by a way in which you are not.

24. Dumery, *Philosophie de la Religion*, II (P.U.F.), p. 286.
25. Tillich, *The Shaking of the Foundations* (New York: Scribner, 1948), pp. 161 ff.
26. Baruzi, *Saint Jean de la Croix et le Problème de l'Expérience Mystique*, 2nd ed. (Paris: Alcan, 1931), p. 535.
27. *Ibid.*, p. 164. When one is devoid of possibilities for sensory re-creation (cf. John of the Cross, *Subida*, Book III, Ch. XXXVIII), this leads to the soul's being brushed in its substance by the loving substance of God (cf. John of the Cross, commentary on Verse IV of the Second Stanza of *Dark Night of the Soul*).
28. John A. T. Robinson, *Honest to God, op. cit.*, p. 28.
29. *Ibid.*, p. 69.
30. *Ibid.*, p. 140.
31. Søren Kierkegaard, *Philosophic Fragments*, trans. by David Swenson, rev. trans. by Howard V. Hong (Princeton: Princeton University Press, 1962), frontispiece; *Concluding Unscientific Postscript, op. cit.*, p. 18.
32. *Ibid.*
33. Dr. Charles Odier, *Les Deux Sources, Consciente et Inconsciente, de la Vie Morale* (Neuchatel: Éditions de la Baconnière), pp. 56-57.
34. *Ibid.*, p. 55.
35. *Ibid.*, p. 59.
36. *Ibid.*, pp. 56-57.
37. *Ibid.*, p. 100.
38. Dumery, *Phénomenologie et Religion, op. cit.*, p. 10. The author speaks more specifically of Judaism here.
39. "The conclusion of belief is not so much a conclusion as a resolution, and it is for this reason that belief excludes doubt." Kierkegaard, *Philosophical Fragments, op. cit.*, p. 104.

40. See Dr. Charles Odier, *Les Deux Sources, Consciente et Inconsciente, de la Vie Morale, op. cit.,* p. 221.

41. On the subject of the philosopher and the sage, see Kojève, *Introduction à la Lecture de Hegel* (N.R.F.), pp. 280-281.

42. Sartre, *The Transcendence of the Ego* trans. by F. Williams and R. Kirkpatrick (New York: Farrar, Strauss and Giroux, 1962), p. 92.

43. *Ibid.,* p. 92.

44. *Ibid.,* p. 48.

45. Baruzi, *Saint Jean de la Croix et le Problème de l'Expérience Mystique, op. cit.,* p. 686.

46. *Ibid.,* p. 11.

47. *Ibid.,* p. 89.

48. *Ibid.,* pp. 123-124.

49. *Ibid.,* p. 371. Italics mine.

50. *Ibid.,* pp. 254-258.

51. *Ibid.,* pp. 500-501.

52. *Ibid.,* p. 685.

53. *Ibid.,* p. 638.

54. Morel, *Le Sens de l'Existence selon Saint Jean de la Croix,* I (Éditions Aubier), p. 19.

55. *Ibid.,* p. 21.

56. *Ibid.,* p. 21.

57. *Ibid.,* p. 30.

58. *Ibid.,* p. 32.

59. *Ibid.,* p. 35.

60. *Ibid.,* p. 36.

61. *Ibid.,* p. 46.

62. *Ibid.,* p. 49.

63. Kierkegaard, *Concluding Unscientific Postscript, op. cit.,* p. 520.

64. Michel Foucault, *Les Mots et les Choses* (N.R.F.), p. 398.

65. Here are the author's exact words: "There is no such thing as a Christian ethics, distinct from human ethics. There are human ethics of lesser and greater degrees of isolation, all of which claim to possess

concretized and deified values and ideals. There is an ethics which is simultaneously a requirement; it exists and does not exist, it must be created and is struggling to produce a man who is not the mystified product of his own products." Francis Jeanson, in "Morale, Metaphysique et Religion," a lecture delivered at the 1966 Conference of Catholic Intellectuals.

66. Merleau-Ponty, *Phenomenology of Perception, op. cit.,* p. XX.

67. *Ibid.,* p. XVI.

68. The words of Francis Jeanson in his lecture, "Morale, Métaphysique et Religion," delivered at the 1966 Conference of Catholic Intellectuals.

69. Lawrence of the Resurrection, *Practice of the Presence of God* (Westwood, N.J.: Revell).

70. Odier, *Les Deux Sources, Consciente et Inconsciente, de la Vie Morale, op. cit.,* p. 100.

71. The differences in our thinking before and after Freud can be clearly seen in the analysis of the parallels between neurosis and religion. *Before* Freud, religious practices would have been readily cleared of suspicion by the simple fact that they contained a meaning. *After* Freud, this fact was no guarantee that the practices were not charged with illusion. Freud felt he could maintain that religion was merely humanity's neurosis. For him religion and neurotic obsession can be explained *in the same terms.* There is a structural analogy between them. Freud found that there is meaning to compulsive acts, and that their "senselessness" is only apparent. With this the principal difference between neurosis and religion disappears, and *neurotic obsession has every bit as much meaning as does a private religion.* In both cases, actions are carried out without consciousness of their meaning, and the motivations which prompt the believer to perform religious *practices* are really *pretexts.* Freud extends the analogy to the level of rules and ceremonies; he notes the *conscientiousness* with which they are carried out, the attentiveness brought to the least detail; he notes the *anxiousness* that accompanies errors or omissions. Prohibition of impulsive acts is supposed to lead to the renunciation of these acts. Thus, all prohibitions in both neurotic obsession and reli-

gious practices are preventive measures designed to suppress acts charged with *unconscious guilt,* and the guilt corresponds to fear of divine punishment. Thus, ritual becomes a compromise, the condition in which such acts become permissible. Carrying this thinking further, we see the Church's marriage ceremony as authorization of an otherwise sinful sexual pleasure.

After analyses of this sort have been made, we cannot talk about religious practices as we did *before.* The purpose of this book has not been to go into such details. This example is enough to indicate the transformation a question has undergone and to point out the new demands for thoroughness and precision which have resulted.